MAIN STREET MAVERICKS

INNOVATION, LEADERSHIP AND A BRIGHT FUTURE FOR MAIN STREET BUSINESSES

JAIME J. IZURIETA

Storyfront
PRESS

ISBN: 979-8-218-40107-8

Table of Contents

Acknowledgments

I am deeply grateful to have reached this milestone with "Main Street Mavericks." This journey has been one of exploration, innovation, and growth, and I owe immense thanks to those who have supported me along the way, especially my friends Jef Buehler, Susan Adelizzi-Schmidt, Kate Giovambattista, and my wife, Lupe.

To the incredible team of proofreaders who meticulously combed through every word, ensuring clarity and coherence, your dedication is truly appreciated. Your insights have undoubtedly refined the quality of this work.

I extend my heartfelt gratitude to the book's designer, Jose Echeverria of Novel Editores, who contributed his expertise and creativity to the realization of this project.

To my readers and supporters, your enthusiasm and engagement inspire me to continue exploring new frontiers of thought, design, and experience creation. Thank you.

Foreword

Sometimes, there's nothing like a good paradigm to help make a little sense out of this crazy world. It also doesn't hurt when it comes to looking at downtown revitalization.

Main Street Mavericks is all about adding some structured insights into how we approach district management and revitalization and focus on working with our small businesses.

Because the fact is not all businesses, no matter how beloved, no matter how awesome their owners might be, are going to succeed. And not all districts are going to succeed either, particularly if they're not investing their finite time, talent, and treasure wisely. Think of this book as a guide to provide some of that wisdom. And by doing so to help reduce the failure rate of both businesses and districts.

I strongly believe that the businesses and districts that do prosper are going to excel at managing the four prosperity values: Economic Value, Place Value, Social Value, and Civic Value. These no doubt sound familiar to followers of the Main Street Approach™, and indeed, those values were adapted from said eponymous approach to the realities of New Jersey some 20 years ago.

On both the individual business and district levels, working towards prosperity is the number one goal. But what is prosperity?

Many people equate prosperity with growth. Prosperity is not growth: Growth by itself is not necessarily a good thing. I think we can all agree that cancer, with its indiscriminate growth, is universally bad. Putting a nuclear cooling tower in a downtown might create hundreds of well-paying jobs and raise a good amount of taxes for the local community. But what's the consequence of that growth? Probably not prosperity.

For me, prosperity is the balance between productivity and fit.

This means finding that sweet spot where the needs of the community, the market, the physical reality of the district, and its governance are well met. Where the Place Value is enhanced by the look and feel of a certain business. Where the Social Value – fun, equity, and access – the business brings to the district is improved. Where the business positively impacts community pride and Civic Value. And of course, where the business is commercially successful for itself, but also elevates the local economy and the district's Economic Value as a whole.

In Main Street Mavericks, the keen insights and paradigms that Jaime shares are hard-won across countries, states, cities, and towns and hundreds of individual business consultations, conversations, and collaborations. They are tools of vocabulary and language that can provide a framework for how districts prioritize the use of resources when it comes to enhancing individual businesses and district prosperity.

Language is important because it helps us envision and understand the complex world in which we exist. It forms the architecture that leads to what we build, where and how we invest our energy, and what we strive to create.

I've had the luck of working with Jaime for several years and in a few different capacities. We've collaborated in both English and Spanish over that time, including more recently discussing the initial "language" that ultimately led to the creation of this book. If you're working in the district management space, I can tell you that his insights are valuable. And that they can help you frame your approach to working with your businesses. And that they can likely help you foster prosperity.

In some ways, this book feels like the start of a process, not the conclusion. Let's face it, district management and downtown revitalization is a pretty rich and chaotic arena. There's always so much changing and going on. That's why a good paradigm can help create a little bit of order.

I love learning. In the process of reading the drafts of Main Street Mavericks, I definitely learned some things, got inspired, and generated a ton of questions. I have a pretty strong hunch that anyone who cares about districts and their businesses and reads this book will grow from it (and do good things with what they learned) as well.

Jef Buehler
Former State Coordinator, Main Street New Jersey

A Prelude to Transformation.

My job is making downtowns and local businesses unforgettable. This journey started years ago when my family acted on a longtime dream to open a bookstore. Their vision sent me on an enlightening path to Buenos Aires to learn the art of infusing magic into commercial spaces so they could sell memories and emotional connections instead of just goods or services. Guiding our group of future booksellers was a well-known designer of legendary bookstores. Miguel Sal, famed for transformative designs from Rome to Singapore, was a pioneer of experiential design, embracing this approach well before it became a recognized term in our industry.

During the study trip, I learned the art of creating spaces that invited curiosity, built connections, and told a story. Selling books was not the most explicit goal. Sal taught about the power of design nuances that many overlook, like the subtle slant of shelves, a small but important detail allowing customers to view books without the inconvenience of kneeling. These lessons transcended the practicalities of design; they were about crafting experiences, about the quiet power of details that transform ordinary spaces into sanctuaries of imagination and learning.

Years later, I would read about Pixar's painstaking work in modeling the home of WALL-E to a point where no one watching the movie could manage to see every object in the room during a scene in which the camera pans through it. They included those anyway because, in director Andrew Stanton's words, "it's the little whispers that speak to the audience."[1]

That was the same level of detail that Miguel Sal talked about. Armed with this knowledge, and a newfound appreciation for the massive impact that design details can make, I returned from Buenos Aires to my then home in Quito, Ecuador. There, I designed our bookshop, *Librería Rayuela*. Named after Julio Cortazar's famed novel, Rayuela was the manifestation of a vision, a space where every shelf, every corner, spoke of a journey and a passion for books. And it was also the repurposed former home of my aunt Monica, the master bookseller.

Almost two decades later, Rayuela still embodies the enduring beauty and charm of its original design and the diligent care for excellent customer service that inspired it. It has become a staple in Quito's independent bookstore scene; it's a beloved haven for book lovers, a place that embodies the spirit of its community. Without any intention of bragging, it remains, to this day, the most beautiful, quaint bookshop in town. I am privileged to have served as Chief Espresso Officer there. My family's journey, from a dream to a community cornerstone, has been a profound part of my life and forms the foundation of the story I will share with you.

Fred Kent, the founder of the Placemaking movement, likes to talk about how one's trajectory leaves a mark on everything it touches. My trajectory has been a blend of diverse ventures, all intertwined by a single, defining thread: a deep-seated passion

[1] Theodore B. Kinni and The Disney Institute, Be Our Guest

for enriching how experiences touch lives. It began with Rayuela, designed as a journey in itself, where every corner and every station along the customer's path was a carefully crafted experience, setting a precedent for all my future endeavors.

Design was all around me, and I could see how things looked better, functioned more properly, and brought happiness to their users. This realization led me to practice my formal training in architecture and urban design. I worked on projects that spanned historic preservation to retail design to local economic development. Each project was a lesson in balancing aesthetics with utility, improving the quality of the interaction between the built environment and its users, and contributing to the communal narrative of the spaces we inhabit.

A decade after creating a community hub with Rayuela, I found myself heading the Smart City division at the municipality of Quito, eventually leading to the foundation of the Office of Urban Mechanics, within the mayor's office. Our mission was to fix the touchpoints where citizens interacted with their local government. We focused on the broken process of street design and created a few iconic projects that are still active today.

My experience with urban mechanics and city planning further expanded when I led a team that contributed to the development of a new city around a university and innovation district. The project was sponsored by the Ecuadorian Ministry of Higher Education, Science and Technology. Besides the infrastructure, technology, and design components, it was a masterclass about the essence of what makes people fall in love with the place they live in.

A logical segue to my trajectory was the establishment of Storefront Mastery as a creative agency with the goal of helping downtown managers make people fall in love with the places they create. My work has led me to challenge local businesses to become champions of beauty and meaningful leisure in their neighborhoods. With unique locations, charmingly quirky offers, human-scaled design, and tailor-made service delivery, these businesses are uniquely positioned to build up their local identity and pride. They contribute immensely to transforming their spaces into coveted destinations.

In numerous instances, however, local business owners overlook opportunities, effectively delaying revitalization efforts. This phenomenon is often attributed to a lack of engagement with available support mechanisms such as grants and technical assistance, but it may lie at the core of how programs are designed and delivered. While some Main Street managers effectively allocate these resources, resulting in successful project completions, there remains a notable frequency of truncated projects, prompting us to reevaluate our underlying assumptions.

A paradigm shift is required in the way we approach the support systems for local businesses, viewing them not merely as beneficiaries but as potential clients. Their engagement – time, attention, and commitment – is the currency in this context. To assist with this commitment, our marketing strategies must transform these businesses into willing clients if we are to maximize existing and future opportunities for growth and prosperity.

As we walk on this journey together, you will discover the key lessons that have shaped my understanding of local economies and their undeniable potential for making people feel welcome, and at peace, and transforming the way they think and see themselves, their town, and their business. Each chapter of this book is crafted to provide insights into how we can revitalize our downtowns and main streets as lively community hubs that offer exceptional experiences and create value for locals and visitors alike. You'll learn the art of creating physical locations that tell stories, invite emotional connections, entice transformations, and are beloved by their communities.

From stories of visionary entrepreneurs to tactical work with local organizations, you'll see how thoughtful design, keen attention to the details of extraordinary hospitality, and a deep understanding of why we love the places we inhabit can transform downtowns. We'll examine the world of local businesses, learning how their unique positions enable them to become beacons of innovation and community engagement. You'll discover how to leverage the strengths of different business types and how strategic support can uplift entire business tiers, contributing to our urban landscapes' civic pride and sense of place.

This book is a compilation of experiences and insights that are meant as a guide and an inspiration for anyone looking to make a meaningful impact in their local community. Whether you're a budding entrepreneur, a seasoned business owner, a city planner, or simply someone who loves their community, these pages are filled with valuable lessons on creating spaces that resonate with people and contribute to the collective narrative of our towns and cities.

With each story and lesson shared, you'll gain a deeper appreciation for the role of innovative design and service delivery in shaping our public spaces and the power of outstanding hospitality in offering unforgettable experiences. As we turn these pages, I invite you to reimagine what our main streets and downtowns could be – energetic, welcoming, and reflective of the unique spirit of their communities.

"Main Street Mavericks" primarily aims to illuminate the extraordinary opportunity that local businesses have to carve out their particular niches and evolve into industry leaders. We start with a detailed taxonomy of Main Street businesses, categorized along three axes, dealing with the quality of their product, the profitability of their business model, and the attractiveness of their service delivery. Each category within these axes encapsulates a vital aspect of the local business landscape, contributing uniquely to the sense of place, identity, and vibrancy of our communities.

In the following chapters, we inquire into the essence of each business category, dissecting their attributes, challenges, and value-adds. We'll explore the lessons taught by Creators, who, with optimal product-market fit, captivate the most attention, bring the most foot traffic, and drive the most sales. We'll uncover how Seekers, given the proper support, can iterate and invigorate their product. We will navigate the journey of Visionary and Drifters, understanding their business models' relative complexity and profitability, and appreciate how Coupler companies, through their creativity and entrepreneurship, can mentor Damper counterparts to improve their design, service delivery, and operations.

Beyond mere classification, we group these businesses into types and then into a tier system that opens the door to specific strategies meant to help each with differentiated attention. This system helps us tailor the support that each one needs to become a stellar destination. The subsequent chapters focus on strategies to harness the strengths of top-tier businesses, uplifting those in lower tiers, and a dual approach to bolster the Attractor tier internally and through local place management organizations.

This journey goes beyond categorizing businesses, exploring the core of local economies, seeking innovative ways to understand their dynamics in main streets, and unlocking their potential to revitalize our downtowns. It is an invitation for every Main Street business to become an attraction, and make an excellent case for people to fall in love with their place.

Let's begin.

Chapter 1. The Landscape of Growth

Every storefront tells a story and is a piece of a larger economic puzzle we're set to solve. In the nuances of how each local business works lies the potential to transform downtown streets into thriving community hubs. And the answer to the riddle of how to maximize the value potential that emerges from the support that place managers can offer.

In my experience with providing design and service advice for local businesses, I've often collaborated with local organizations and government agencies on grant programs. Despite the opportunities, which include non-refundable facade upgrade funding, a significant and recurring challenge has been the reluctance of business owners to take advantage of these grants, effectively leaving resources untapped. This book aims to tackle this issue head-on. We propose targeted strategies to redesign these programs and enhance the capacity of business owners, ensuring they fully leverage the available support to improve their storefronts.

Local business owners often find themselves overwhelmed with everyday burdens, such as tax planning, compliance with local, state, and federal rules and regulations, staff management, or procurement. These activities take the lion's share of store owners' time and prevent them from focusing on their business's public face – the product, customer touchpoints, design, and service delivery.

As much as business in the past was about capturing the customer's money, today it's about capturing their time and making sure it is well spent in the company of our brand. The design of the in-store experience and how customers interact with it is a vital component of this effort.

In the current market landscape, the act of delivering products and services has evolved into an experience in its own right, distinguishing itself as a unique product. Independent, local businesses frequently possess a distinct advantage in excelling at this facet, transforming each interaction – be it through digital platforms or in physical store environments – into an engaging and memorable journey for the customer.

In this chapter, we examine the definition and implications of growth for small businesses in main streets and downtowns, establishing a foundation for the book's primary argument. Our analysis suggests that the outcomes of support strategies for local businesses can be substantially optimized. To carry on this optimization, we need a detailed understanding of the distinct characteristics of different local business types and the application of insights gleaned from high-performing enterprises. The strategic adaptation of support mechanisms, aligned with the specific needs of each business type, emerges as a critical factor in driving effective growth and development.

In the face of numerous challenges – a sluggish economy, soaring inflation, escalating debt, fierce competition from large retail chains and online giants, and often restrictive local regulations – the path to growth for local businesses demands a strategic outlook. It calls for a profound understanding of their unique strengths and an in-depth analysis of their customer base. Identifying niches where a physical location becomes an advantage is key. When local businesses combine superb physical storefronts with outstanding service, they craft exceptional experiences that resonate with customers.

In our observation of local business trends, we find a significant shift towards prioritizing efficient service delivery at competitive prices. This shift has led to the commodification of services, a process where unique or differentiated products become more standardized and interchangeable in the eyes of consumers. As a result, customers increasingly gravitate towards companies that excel in efficiency, logistics, and finance-oriented models. Online retail giants like Amazon or Alibaba and large chain retailers such as Walmart or Target, which exemplify these characteristics, are particularly benefiting from this trend. Reports predict that in 2023, 75% of consumers are expected to spend more with online retailers, a trend driven by the convenience and efficiency these outlets offer[2].

Online retailers and large chains have the carrying capacity to grow their market share exponentially, due to economic factors well beyond what local economic development actors can change. They are thus capable of offering convenience at impressively low prices, on account of their larger market share. E-commerce is thought to reach $1.6 trillion by 2027[3]. This often leads to a

[2] Mirakl, Consumer Preferences in the Digital-First Economy

[3] FTI Consulting 2023 Online Retail Report

homogenization of customer service, to meet basic demands of very large segments of the population.

The challenge these commercial behemoths face, despite the growing use of technological toolkits such as Artificial Intelligence (AI) or Augmented Reality (AR) to provide models, predictions, and shopping experiences, is to provide memorable moments and transformative experiences beyond the purely transactional aspect of shopping. Local, independent businesses are naturally positioned to do this.

From this new context, the concept of "Experience Economy," as coined by Joe Pine and James Gilmore in their seminal book of the same name, emerges as a new paradigm of service delivery. Experiences, as defined by Pine and Gilmore, are *"memorable events that engage each individual in an inherently personal way."*[4]

According to forecasts, about 72% of Gen-Z customers say they would switch to new brands if they offer personalized shopping experiences[5]. The trend in both brick-and-mortar and online retailers is towards staging engaging, memorable experiences. This evolution poses a significant challenge for local businesses. No longer competing on fair terms, small outfits find it increasingly difficult to survive on thin margins and to compete in price and novelty. Their lifeline relies on recognizing the need to evolve beyond services, to offer outstanding design and service delivery that captivate customers' attention, time, and heart, aligning with values and supporting meaningful missions. In sum: providing fantastic experiences.

---

[4] Journal of Shopper Research, 2017: J. Pine and J. Gilmore, "Distinctive Experiences"

[5] FTI Consulting 2023 Online Retail Report

The Experience Economy isn't just on the horizon – it's here, already dominating the hospitality, entertainment, and high-end commercial sectors. It presents a unique opportunity for Main Street businesses to polish their value proposition and become incomparable in a domain where main streets and downtowns can truly excel.

What Growth Means

Our society is obsessed with numbers. We judge things on their size and reach, and not so much on their quality. We often find ourselves measuring success through towering buildings, sizable investments, venue capacity, or stock price. This fixation extends to how we view businesses, judging them by their market caps and fretting over single-digit sales increases. However, this metric of magnitude tells only part of the story, especially when we turn our gaze to main streets and downtowns.

In the heart of our communities, local businesses operate on a different scale. These quaint shops, cozy eateries, and neighborhood coffee houses measure their success in the strength of their community ties, the loyalty of their customers, and their contributions to local vibrancy. They exist as stakeholders in the prosperity of their neighborhoods, bringing unique charm and character to their locales. Yet, these businesses are not isolated from broader economic currents such as shifts in real estate markets, overarching economic trends, and burgeoning competition.

Redefining growth in this local context shifts the focus from purely financial achievements to a different measure of success.

The pristine balance sheets or stellar financial health might help. The core of what growth is in this context, however, is in the collaborative creation of value and supporting a thriving community. Growth for these businesses is seen in their ability to contribute to a triple bottom line: sustaining financial viability, lifting community wellbeing, and nurturing overall neighborhood vitality.

Our vision of growth for independent, local businesses is rooted in their ability to become integral, beloved parts of their community's life. This paradigm advocates for a strategy where financial robustness is achieved in harmony with, rather than at the expense of, community welfare. We see main streets and downtowns as the beating hearts of our towns and cities.

What Growth May Look Like

We have gone over the challenges that independent, local businesses have, which often make their operations unsustainable. High overhead costs, insufficiently developed value propositions, and less than magical product-market fit are often compensated by offering an unreachable standard of service delivery. The result is a low survival rate.

The alternative is a recognition that the power of design, marketing, and experience are inherent to downtowns, main streets, and their local businesses. Their human scale, personalized offer, and strong identity transform communities into destinations and put places on the map. Growth for these businesses means elevating their offer to occupy a unique niche: unrepeatable, tailored, location-based experiences.

Our journey through this new economy will deepen our understanding of these business categories and lead to a strategic focus on the key aspects that distinguish the businesses that drive the most foot traffic and sales. We will learn how top-tier brands have crafted targeted strategies and we will apply those lessons to bolster strong local players as they step into the Experience Economy, transforming them into engines of broader economic growth and community connection.

By the end of this exploration, our goal is to provide economic developers, urban planners, and local business advocates with valuable insights to transform Main Street into a realm of extraordinary experiences and unparalleled hospitality. We're set to unveil strategies that animate the most powerful aspects and robust opportunities of these businesses.

The mission is straightforward: to ignite a renaissance in downtowns, turning them into the epicenters of community and commerce, where every street corner whispers an invitation to an adventure yet to be written.

Chapter 2. Main Street is a Festival and Every Store is a Stage

Main Street is not just a location; it's a stage for unforgettable experiences. The success of local businesses in a context of exponentially growing technology and convenience relies on their ability to offer the emotional connection that neither online shopping nor large, impersonal chain stores can. The present chapter explores how every Main Street business, irrespective of its category, can significantly benefit from adopting a hospitality-centric perspective, transforming every customer interaction into a memorable event.

We find ourselves in a world where, as Joe Pine and Jim Gilmore brilliantly encapsulate in "The Experience Economy," "work is theater and each business is a stage." This insightful quote, paraphrased in this chapter's title, lays the groundwork for our exploration of how outstanding customer service and a hospitality mindset for every local business can be instrumental in reinventing and revitalizing our downtowns. It reminds us that companies are commercial entities and a profitable way to design their service looks at every interaction as a performance, every product as a prop, and every customer as an engaged audience member.

In the process of transforming Main Street businesses into hospitality-centric destinations, the principles championed by

Will Guidara in his book "Unreasonable Hospitality," have a significant impact. His concept revolves around the idea that each interaction with the customer is an opportunity to surpass the customer's expectations. When service goes out of its way to offer unexpected pleasures and thoughtful gestures, businesses create a lasting impression, turning casual visitors into loyal patrons. Business owners in the Main Street space, where the most significant touchpoint is the street-facing store, need to acknowledge that they are in the Hospitality business, regardless of what their business does.

A cornerstone of this transformation is the creation of deep emotional connections with customers, a principle that lies at the heart of the Disney Institute's "Be Our Guest." The magic of Disney's system is in making every guest feel uniquely special and valued. Main Street businesses can mirror this by cultivating an environment where customers feel genuinely cared for and appreciated, turning every visit into a personally meaningful experience.

Starbucks stands as a fantastic example of this approach. Since its founding in 1971, they steadily changed consumer preferences by offering an alternative to the conventional coffee shop experience. From its initial moment of expansion in the early 90s, Starbucks has continually evolved its model to maintain a deep, personal connection with its customers. As the brand grew to a massive scale, needing several adjustments to standardize processes, there was a recognition of the need to reinvent and offer something even more exclusive and immersive. The introduction of the Starbucks Reserve™ Roastery was a clever response to the massification of the Starbucks brand. The new brand, aimed at a higher target group, revisited several of the original tenets of design, storytelling, and sophistication, but with a more elaborate, experience-led delivery of services.

The Starbucks Reserve™ Roastery is an ambitious expansion of Starbucks' original vision, an homage to the craft and journey of coffee, with an inspired brand that made its mark in Milan, in one of the toughest coffee markets in the world. The Starbucks roasteries are stages where baristas perform to offer a heightened, immersive experience, as much as they are serving coffee. They represent a return to the roots of coffee brewing, a celebration of the artistry and emotional resonance of coffee-making.

Through its roastery model, Starbucks demonstrates how even a global brand can innovate to offer small-scale, high-end experiences that resonate with the evolving tastes and expectations of customers. It exemplifies the power of a hospitality-centric approach in adapting and thriving, showcasing that the principles of memorable, immersive experiences are vital at every scale of operation.

Attention to detail is another lesson drawn from both Guidara and Disney. Making the finer aspects of the experience the focal point that drives design and service delivery can make any ordinary business an extraordinary one. Whether it's the ambiance, customer service, or the quality of products. Paying close attention to detail demonstrates a commitment to excellence that customers recognize and appreciate.

Shinola, a Detroit-based brand synonymous with quality and craftsmanship, was built from the ashes of a city plagued with development issues but ready for revitalization. Shinola offers products that resonate with a story of resurgence and community spirit. Initially focused on meticulously crafted watches and leather goods, Shinola has become a symbol of pride and quality in American manufacturing. As the brand expanded, it retained its core ethos but sought new ways to deepen its connection with customers and the narrative it represents.

In response to its growth, Shinola introduced experiential elements into its retail spaces, transforming them into stages. These spaces became emblems of their commitment to craftsmanship and community. Inspired by the rich industrial history of Detroit, Shinola's stores offer customers a window into the meticulous process of creating their products. From watchmaking demonstrations to showcasing the careful art of leather craftsmanship, these spaces function as interactive galleries where customers can witness the dedication and skill that goes into every product.

The evolution of Shinola's retail experience exemplifies how a brand can grow while maintaining a solid connection to its roots and community. Their stores are cultural hubs that celebrate the city's heritage and the brand's commitment to quality and craftsmanship. They have harnessed the power of storytelling to captivate, and of experiential retail to engage their customers with the brand's narrative. The journey of interacting with Shinola makes the customer a part of Detroit's transformation into the poster child of grassroots urban regeneration.

Personalization, as a preeminent theme in "Unreasonable Hospitality," is essential for upgrading experiences. Its application extends beyond product customization to the very environment in which businesses operate. This concept is exemplified in services and products and manifested in the unique store experiences created by companies like Warby Parker, Dyson, Aesop, and Purple. Aesop, in particular, demonstrates this through its distinctive store designs, each crafted by top designers to ensure that every location offers a unique and immersive experience. The fastidious attention to the individuality of each store underlines the importance of personalization in creating a memorable brand identity.

For Main Street businesses, this approach translates into opportunities to make each customer feel uniquely valued, whether through remembering a regular's favorite product, tailoring services, or simply greeting customers by name. Warby Parker's personalized eyewear choices, Dyson's adaptable technology for different living environments, Aesop's commitment to distinct store aesthetics, and Purple's focus on individual sleep preferences are prime examples of how personal touches can provide an unforgettable experience.

These strategies, going beyond just products to include the overall customer environment, demonstrate how Main Street businesses can leverage personalization to create unique, memorable experiences. Such a degree of personalization sets businesses apart in a competitive market and forges deeper connections with customers.

Embracing exceptional hospitality is a transformative process that enables businesses and local organizations to contribute immensely to the pride and identity of their communities. This section has aimed to inspire local leaders, place managers, and business owners to see every visitor and customer interaction as an opportunity for extraordinary hospitality, setting businesses apart and enriching the vibrancy and prosperity of the entire district.

In this transformation, the evolution of Starbucks into the Starbucks Reserve™ Roastery and Shinola's experiential retail strategy stand as testaments to the power of reimagining customer interactions. These examples illustrate how businesses can evolve while maintaining a deep connection with customers through innovative experiences. Starbucks' transition from a coffee shop to an immersive coffee journey and Shinola's transformation of retail spaces into cultural hubs highlight the importance of storytelling in creating unique, memorable experiences.

At the time of writing, there was one buzzword that seemingly guided every single marketing campaign. Storytelling, employed successfully by Disney, Starbucks, and Shinola, is a very effective method of communication; it allows the creation of enchanting, transformative narratives that set the mood for how we experience places.

By weaving compelling narratives into their products or services, Main Street businesses cease to be purely transactional and become experiential; they invite customers into an immersive story that enriches every interaction. The following section will look deeper into how storytelling can be harnessed by Main Street businesses to create their magic, turning every customer interaction into a memorable journey and nurturing lasting bonds within the community.

Chapter 3. Narratives That Thrive

Stories are the architecture of our lives; they shape our experiences and mold our perceptions. In the modern business ecosystem, storytelling has ascended as a very influential toolkit. Its brilliance is revealed in how successful companies have shifted their communications strategies to sell the emotional connection that stories can achieve, as opposed to listing the benefits of their products. In this chapter, we will explore how storytelling can build deep emotional connections and will demonstrate how it transcends its buzzword status to help us set the playing field for truly immersive experiences.

We will learn from the insights of neuroscientists and inventor Paul Zak, as we unravel the neuroscience that explains the power of stories. Understanding the mechanics of how narratives can profoundly influence customer behavior and perception provides a foundation for constructing stories that effectively capture and maintain audience attention, supporting deeper connections with the brand.

Drawing from the expertise of Margaret Kerrison, an experienced Disney Imagineer, we uncover the art of constructing rich, immersive worlds through storytelling. Her wisdom guides us in developing narratives that transport customers beyond the ordinary into experiences that are as boundless as they are unforgettable. Especially relevant for

Main Street businesses, narratives hoist businesses above the transactions they make, creating escapades that etch lasting memories in customers' minds.

We also glean insights into authenticity from Joe Pine and Jim Gilmore, acclaimed authors of "The Experience Economy." Their teachings illuminate the profound impact of authenticity in storytelling, emphasizing the need for narratives that resonate with truth and integrity. Authentic stories are spellbinding and engaging. They solidify trust and credibility with the audience, as they reflect the genuine heart and soul of the business.

Our mission is to transform storytelling from a common buzzword into a dynamic, impactful tool for Main Street businesses. The aim is to equip these businesses with the capacity to craft immersive stories that are engaging and authentic, and reflective of their unique brand ethos. This comprehensive approach to storytelling is set to revolutionize customer interactions, elevating them from simple transactions to profound, meaningful experiences that resonate long after the moment has passed.

My friend Edna, an immigrant like me, who arrived in the US from Uganda, is an inspiring figure who transformed her homewares, gift, and antique shop into a community hub. Deeply rooted in each detail in the public-facing parts of her store is a belief in authenticity, a principle that Edna embraced wholeheartedly. Every item in her shop carries a story, a narrative thread connecting it to its origins, creators, or journey to her storefront. Will Guidara's philosophy encourages the creation of engaging narratives around products and services, transforming every customer interaction into a part of a larger, compelling story. This storytelling aspect is particularly potent for Main Street businesses such as Edna's Papillon & Co., which often have rich histories and strong community ties.

In our initial discussions with Edna, we drew inspiration from Eataly's model, where storytelling is a craft perfected over time. Eataly, known for its exquisite Italian products, goes beyond mere commerce; it weaves narratives of artisans and their painstaking methods of crafting cheese and cold cuts into every product. This technique showcases stories that give significance to each product while paying homage to its origins and the hands that crafted it. For Edna, this method presented a blueprint for transforming her store into a narrative-rich space.

When Edna began applying these concepts, she focused on both the stories behind the products and their presentation. The packaging became a canvas for these narratives, striking a fabulous first impression and inviting customers into the story.

In Paul Zak's framework, the impact of storytelling focuses on the interplay of neurotransmitters. The components of immersion, as conceptualized by Zak, hinge, in his words, on "first get my attention, then give me a reason to care."

Getting attention refers to the immediate, powerful effect that an immersive experience has on an individual. Typically characterized by emotional, cognitive, and sometimes behavioral responses, this initial engagement is driven by dopamine, a neurotransmitter that triggers excitement and interest when we encounter something novel or rewarding.

Dopamine is part of our hunter-gatherer brain's behavior of pointing us to things that might be of service. Since it is associated with the feeling of pleasure an individual feels when they are captivated by something, this immediate response is vital for capturing attention in storytelling, making the content appealing and emotionally stimulating.

Long-term engagement, on the other hand, is about the lasting effect of the experience. Oxytocin, another neurotransmitter released during deeper, more meaningful interactions, creating trust and emotional bonds, has a profound effect on how well the experience sticks in the person's memory and triggers a transformation. These chemical processes in the brain can influence people's thoughts or behaviors over time and continue to engage them even after the initial encounter.

Both components working together create experiences that shift the user's perspective and trigger a transformation.

In practical applications, these neurochemical processes can be leveraged to create compelling narratives in business and marketing. By understanding and utilizing the mechanisms of dopamine and oxytocin release, storytellers can craft experiences that grab attention quickly and also build a lasting connection.

In Edna's store, each item's packaging, pairing, and location might serve as an introduction to its story. Customers would first be captivated by the visual appeal and then drawn deeper by the narrative, thus creating a more immersive experience.

This combination of aesthetic allure and rich storytelling created a multi-sensory experience. Customers underwent a personal transformation when they purchased a piece of culture, a fragment of tradition, and the stories that go with it. It was an experience that stayed with them, making the product more than just an object but a token of a larger, more immersive narrative.

The journey of finding authenticity in Edna's shop can be seen as a delicate interplay between the overarching narrative of the store and the individual stories of each piece. While many items naturally come with their own histories, some lack this feature. In these instances, Edna was encouraged to employ a bit of creative license to "make up a cousin" – a metaphor for crafting a story that, though not factual, still resonates with the essence of authenticity.

This concept of crafting narratives is akin to a playwright creating a web of characters and plots. Each item in Edna's store becomes a character with its own backstory, contributing to the larger narrative of the shop. The store itself is like a stage where these narratives play out, each item adding depth and texture to the overall experience. By attaching stories to products without a known history, Edna is building up the in-store experience with a richer context.

Drawing upon Margaret Kerrison's insights in 'Immersive Design for Real and Imagined Worlds,' we understand how imagined narratives can significantly enhance the retail experience. Kerrison advocates for the creation of stories that transport customers to both natural and fantastical realms, enriching their interaction with products.

These narratives, woven into the fabric of the shopping environment, could invite customers into a world where each item holds a unique tale, be it historical or fantastical. The goal is to turn a simple shopping trip into an exploratory adventure, deepening the emotional resonance and memorability of the experience. Embracing both the real and the imagined allows retailers like Edna, as well as other business owners in the hospitality or service areas, to craft a captivating, story-rich atmosphere that intrigues and delights their customers.

The smaller narratives of individual items, whether factual or crafted, meld with the larger narrative of the store, creating a dynamic and engaging environment. The magic of Edna's shop lies in the balance between truth and fiction, history and imagination. It's a space where stories live and breathe, inviting customers to be a part of something more significant than the products they purchase.

Margaret Kerrison's teachings provide a solid foundation for the crafted narratives in Edna's store. The creation of rich, authentic, detailed environments, whether real or imagined, that are armed with a solid narrative and stating a clear goal for how it will enhance the users' lives enhances engagement and immersion.

If every Main Street business is a hospitality business, it is also an Experiential one. Understanding the intricacies of this statement can help creative business owners and designers craft stories for items that lack one, as these narratives contribute to a more captivating and immersive shopping experience. It means that by default, Main Streets are uniquely positioned to be destinations, and the way to manage destinations is by being hosts. When visitors arrive and they experience great hospitality, they reward the businesses and the place by patronizing and spending their time there. The hospitality component kicks in when businesses design both real and imaginative components within a retail experience and create a unique, memorable environment that resonates deeply with customers.

A holistic product presentation with attached storytelling has become a cornerstone of Edna's business philosophy. It highlighted the importance of every element in the retail experience, from the first visual impression to the unfolding of the product's story.

Chapter 4. The Spectrum of Local Business

Imagine your downtown as a theater, where each business, from cozy cafés to lively boutiques, plays a part in the "sidewalk ballet" of local growth and community engagement. Now, envision yourself clad in walking shoes, donning a bright safety vest emblazoned with your local BID logo, clipboard in hand, tallying tree pits, and blade signs under the summer sun.

This scene encapsulates my Summer of 2022 experience with the Montclair Center BID in Montclair, New Jersey, working on the Mercator Project to map the entire business ecosystem of the district. Our task included collecting detailed data on every ground-floor commercial space in the district. This area is bustling with nearly 450 sidewalk-facing businesses, plus several more located inside buildings and on upper floors. The data we gathered is decisive for the BID's strategic planning. It aids in attracting key businesses, identifying effective business clusters, collaborating with property and business owners to minimize vacancies, and devising marketing strategies to draw visitors and investment to the town. This project also marked a significant technological leap for the BID, culminating in the development of an innovative digital dashboard along with software startup Urality. This tool streamlines public space maintenance, stakeholder support, marketing, and internal operations, enhancing overall efficiency.

The effort invested during that summer was substantial, but the value of the information now at the BID's disposal is immense. Similarly, collecting the data required for implementing the proposition of 'Main Street Mavericks' is no desk job. It demands some on-the-ground action, perhaps even pacing Main Street in a bright green vest with a clipboard in hand. Yet, the outcomes far outweigh the effort. Speaking from experience, the hot summer sun can be unforgiving, but the rewards of contributing to the exponential increase in value for Main Street are irreplaceable and immensely fulfilling. Building the capacity to focus the support that each local business gets, increasing their commitment to the district, and engaging their contribution to lift the entire ecosystem sounds like a good bounty.

The book you have in your hands is the result of my expedition into the heart of what makes people fall in love with their downtowns. On that expedition, I learned that the success or failure of local businesses exists along a spectrum. It is not binary. Identifying where each business is along the spectrum confers us the power to make more informed decisions, provide more focused support, and drive better results and returns on our investment.

As we dive into the groundwork to make sense of the spectrum and locate businesses along it, we'll categorize local businesses into three distinct axes that cover the three big areas of a business' operation: the product Focus Axis, measuring how "Creators" and "Seekers" meet the demands of their market; the Value Proposition Axis, exploring how "Visionary" businesses succeed in creating profitable and efficient business models, versus "Drifter" ones, which need more definition of values and goals, a solid path to profitability, and more commitment to delivering excellent products; and the Brand Cohesion Axis, which is a function of whether a business's service is well designed and its daily operations are efficient, and where "Coupler" and "Damper" businesses compete for customers' attention.

Each axis represents a different act in this performance, showcasing the diverse personalities and roles these businesses play. Understanding where a business stands at the intersection of these axes is the first step for tailoring effective support strategies.

Local organizations can offer more precise, impactful support by assessing where each business lies in a matrix that rates its product, profit, and operations. Whether it's the trailblazing café bringing a fresh vibe to the street or the heritage bookstore preserving the community's narrative, pinpointing their position at the crossroads of these categories enables us to develop targeted interventions that resonate with their unique needs and aspirations and amplifies the outcomes by elevating the visibility and attractiveness of the entire place.

This journey goes beyond mere categorization; it's a fun, insightful, and eye-opening exploration of how local economies thrive and evolve. Each business, big or small, is a stage where shopkeepers, attendants, servers and every other worker performs a daily play. They help customers craft memorable experiences with the stories they tell, making the downtown experience unforgettable.

The Product Focus Axis: Crafting the Magic

This axis measures Product-market fit, as it refers to a scenario where a company's product or service meets the demands and needs of its target market effectively. It is achieved when a business offers something that resonates strongly with a particular market segment, resulting in high customer satisfaction and strong sales. A deep focus on creating a product that fits perfectly into a market niche, will address the specific problems, needs, or desires of customers and create a vehicle for relieving a pain point.

Finding resonance with an audience that feels their pain point has been solved typically involves a process of continuous iteration and feedback. Companies start by identifying a target market and understanding its needs and preferences. They then develop a minimum viable product (MVP) to test in the market. Based on customer feedback, companies make necessary adjustments to the product to better meet the market's needs. This cycle of testing, feedback, and adjustment is repeated until the product resonates strongly with the target audience, indicating that product-market fit has been achieved.

When a business achieves product-market fit, its offerings seamlessly resonate with the market, paving the way for enduring growth and prosperity. These businesses are aptly termed Creators, as they have successfully aligned their products with market demands. On the other hand, businesses still striving to find their footing and connect effectively with their target audience fall into the category of Seekers.

Creators: Making Main Street Spectacular

Creators epitomize the essence of innovation and adaptation in the heart of local economies. These businesses, established or emerging local legends, have masterfully achieved an optimal product-market fit through an intensive process of prototyping, iteration, and market feedback. Their entrepreneurial spirit captivates the local community and works to garner recognition beyond regional boundaries, making them key players in defining the downtown's identity.

These establishments are known for their unique, bespoke products or services, drawing significant attention and inspiring ancillary economic activities. The demand for their products infuses the market with vitality, and their presence elicits a positive response from consumers, contributing significantly to the overall happiness and vibrancy of downtown areas. Creators stand in sharp contrast to larger, impersonal retailers by offering novel, distinctive experiences in shopping, dining, and services. This uniqueness sets them apart in the marketplace, creating a distinct brand presence.

These trailblazing entities invest considerable effort in identifying and maintaining an optimal product-market fit, placing them at the pinnacle of their respective sectors. This strategic positioning enables them to carve out a niche in the market effectively, attracting customers who seek premium and unique experiences on Main Street.

Creators are catalysts for transformation and growth in the heart of towns and cities, and their influence extends beyond immediate commercial success. They are a major contributor to shaping the character and narrative of Main Street, blending traditional values with innovative approaches. Their success stories inspire other businesses and elevate the overall standard and appeal of Main Street, setting a benchmark for excellence and encouraging a culture of ambition and forward-thinking.

Seekers: Navigating the Challenges of Changing Markets

Offering a product that fully meets the demand is the cornerstone of a successful business. Reaching the stage of optimal product-market fit is a process of iteration in which a minimum viable product is tested on the market, feedback is incorporated, and modifications are made until the market adopts it naturally.

Markets change, so maintaining a good fit requires constant checks. Businesses that reach an average fit may stay in the market long enough, supported by a strong organization and agile, active service and daily operations, but need to carry on the iterative process.

Seekers in the Main Street business landscape embody businesses still in a quest to find their footing in the dynamic market. They represent the challenging side of entrepreneurship, where the journey to achieving a solid product-market fit is ongoing and often fraught with obstacles. These businesses, characterized by their inconsistent resonance with market needs and preferences, need to fine-tune the prototyping-iteration process to stay relevant and appealing to their target audience.

At the core of the Seeker's challenge is the concept of product-market fit – the degree to which a product satisfies strong market demand. Seekers often find themselves misaligned with their market's needs and desires, a gap that arises from various factors such as shifts in consumer behavior, technological advancements, or evolving cultural trends. The misalignment leads to a diminishing customer base and a struggle to adapt to the changing landscape of consumer expectations.

At first glance, the struggle of Seekers seems like a matter of putting in more effort or financial investment. In reality, it's a condition that requires the will and the time to go through a thorough prototyping-iteration cycle and revised marketing strategies. For some, embracing new technologies, reimagining the product from scratch, or exploring different market segments could be the way forward. Without such strategic adaptation and realignment, Seekers risk continuing on a downward trajectory, regardless of their efforts or investments.

The Seeker category encapsulates a wide range of businesses, from traditional brick-and-mortar stores grappling with the digital revolution to restaurants and service providers challenged by changing consumer lifestyles and preferences. These businesses often need to revisit earlier phases of the business life cycle before they can make a significant shift in philosophy and mindset.

For Main Street's Seeker businesses, the path to transformation and relevance in a competitive market lies in embracing change and innovation. By actively seeking feedback, focusing on experimentation, and being open to redefining their product, these businesses can begin to align more closely with their market.

Seekers' experiences and struggles on Main Street serve as a reminder of the dynamic nature of markets and the importance of agility and responsiveness in business. Their story highlights the ongoing need for businesses to adapt, evolve, and continually seek a deeper connection with their customers' changing needs and desires.

Classification Criteria for Creators and Seekers

The analytical framework delineated in "Main Street Mavericks" dissects local businesses through a tripartite axis system, offering distinct perspectives based on their market fit, profitability, and service delivery efficacy. The challenge that emerges is how to accurately categorize each entity. Traditional survey methodologies, when they manage to get in the bandwidth of overworked small business owners, often suffer from respondent bias, thereby compromising data integrity. Conversely, soliciting detailed financial records and internal business metrics might be perceived as overly intrusive. To circumvent these limitations, this section – replicated for each axis – proposes a robust set of Key Performance Indicators (KPIs). These KPIs are designed to objectively position each Main Street business within the specified axis, ensuring a comprehensive and unbiased evaluation.

To categorize businesses as 'Creators' or 'Seekers' along the product-market fit axis through observable metrics, the following seven Key Performance Indicators (KPIs) are employed. The rating system is binary, which means the business will either be a Creator or a Seeker, depending on whether they have more "Highs" than "Lows".

- Foot Traffic: Quantifying the number of customers entering a business provides a direct indicator of its market appeal. Creators are local anchors and typically attract higher foot traffic compared to Seekers.
- Social Media Presence and Activity: Evaluating the frequency of posts, level of customer engagement, and follower growth on platforms like Instagram or Facebook to measure a business's market resonance. Creators often have a more active and engaged social media presence.
- Local Market Presence: Assessing the visibility of a business in local media, community events, and collaborations. Creators are usually more prominent in local markets, participating actively in community events and collaborations.
- Customer Queue and Wait Times: Observing the length of customer queues and wait times can be an indicator of demand. Longer queues and wait times are often associated with better product-market fit.
- External Reviews and Ratings: Analyzing ratings and reviews on platforms like Google, Yelp, or TripAdvisor can provide insights into customer satisfaction and market fit. Higher ratings and positive reviews are characteristic of Creator businesses.
- Visual Merchandising and Storefront Appeal: Assessing the attractiveness and upkeep of a business's physical appearance, including window displays and general cleanliness, can indicate its market appeal. Creators tend to invest more in creating an appealing storefront.

- Variety and Freshness of Offerings: Observing the range and novelty of products or services offered to determine a business's ability to innovate and adapt to market trends.

An example business in the Creator-Seeker spectrum is **Papillon & Co.**, a home, gift, and antique shop business located in Metuchen, NJ. It has a visibly growing foot traffic, with lots of in-house produced events that circulate heavily on their social media. They are beloved by locals, who participate actively in their offerings, ranging from Murder Mysteries to Art Pop-ups and community dinners. They keep customer service close and personal and have a vast majority of positive reviews. They are constantly improving their displays and arrangements to increase the appeal of the storefront, and constantly bring new unique items to the market. Papillon&Co. qualifies as a **Creator**.

Foot Traffic	H
Social Media Presence and Activity	H
Local Market Presence	H
Customer Queue and Wait Times	L
External Reviews and Ratings	H
Visual Merchandising and Storefront Appeal	H
Variety and Freshness of Offering	H

An Attractive Main Street Ecosystem

Creators, with their magnetic spirit, are decisive in shaping Main Street into a lively and attractive destination. Their creativity and willingness to constantly experiment to optimize their fit in the market bring new life and energy, drawing customers and revitalizing the area.

In a Main Street ecosystem, facilitating collaborative encounters between Creators, with their optimal product-market fit and innovative approaches, and Seekers, who struggle to align their offerings with market needs, can be beneficial in sharing lessons about the iterative process.

Partnerships that take advantage of a mentoring relationship can translate insights, experiences, and strategies into action, enabling Seekers to refine their products and business models more effectively and elevating the playing field for all.

This collaborative dynamic on Main Street has the potential to revolutionize its overall landscape. By transforming challenges into opportunities for innovation and growth, such cooperation aids individual businesses while it uplifts the entire community.

These two categories focus solely on product-market fit. Complementary axes assess additional aspects of the entrepreneurial mindset, which will aid place managers in determining a business's readiness to adapt and meet market demands effectively.

The Core of Downtown experiences

The Creators-Seekers spectrum offers a dynamic view of Main Street's business realm. Creators are those remarkable entities that have expertly navigated the market, achieving an optimal product-market fit. They are innovators and trendsetters, fueling local economies with their unique, high-demand offerings and leading the way toward the Experience Economy. Their impact in drawing customers and creating a distinct local identity is profound. Preferred by their local and even regional markets, they are the core of downtown experiences.

On the other end, Seekers represent businesses still striving to find their market niche. These entities face challenges due to a misalignment with current market demands and require strategic realignment and innovation to stay relevant. The Product-Market Fit axis, therefore, measures the diverse business dynamics on Main Street, highlighting the disparity in market adaptation and the potential for growth and change.

This exploration sets the stage for the upcoming section on the Visionary-Drifter axis, where we'll understand the interplay between innovation and consistency in organizational blueprints. As we segue into the next part of our journey, we will further illuminate how experiential, customer-focused strategies are redefining the vibrancy and resilience of our towns and cities.

Value Proposition Axis: Sustaining the Magic

Visionary Businesses: Catalysts of Economic Transformation

Visionary businesses are the spearheads of Main Street's economic landscape. Characterized by a growth- and abundance mindset, they continuously seek out new opportunities, infusing the local economy with innovation and vitality.

They are engines of innovation and vitality and exemplify the ability to evolve their original value propositions into profitable and sustainable business models. These businesses are adept at identifying and capitalizing on emerging market trends, often expanding their reach by opening new locations, diversifying their product and service offerings, meticulously crafting or maintaining their brand and service models, and partnering with local makers, designers, and strategic allies to improve their offerings.

Visionary businesses' value creation, profitability, and ability to strengthen supply chains and local partnerships are a major force in propelling economic development and setting a pace for the local business community to follow. Their success lies in the agile and successful adaptation of their profit mechanisms while contributing significantly to local economic growth.

These enterprises are iconic examples of adaptability and progress, often serving as inspiration for other businesses in the area to embrace a more expansive outlook. Whether it's a small artisanal bakery that has successfully expanded to supply regional cafes or a local tech start-up scaling its innovative services to a broader market, Visionary businesses demonstrate the potential and rewards of embracing change and growth.

Their success stories highlight the transformative impact that such businesses can have on the entire Main Street ecosystem, encouraging a culture of ambition and forward-thinking that is essential for thriving in today's competitive market.

Drifters: Navigating Challenges in a Changing Economy

In Main Street's diverse ecosystem, Drifter businesses play an often underappreciated part. They are typically small-scale, family-operated ventures, vital in areas where mainstream job opportunities are scarce. Their conventional business models, primarily focused on maintaining existing operations, face significant challenges in adapting to a demanding market.

Drifters face significant challenges due to their predictable organizational behavior, needing help to keep pace with market dynamics, rising operational costs, consumer preferences, and technological advancements. Although they are valued community assets, they find themselves at a critical crossroads where adaptation is necessary for survival and relevance in the lively environment of Main Street.

For instance, a local dry cleaner may maintain a loyal customer base but not broaden its services, or a family-run convenience store might offer essential goods but need more modernization or diversity in its offerings.

A pressing challenge for Drifters is to evolve their operations to remain viable while maintaining their traditional values and the community ties that have supported them over the years. This process calls for a change in business practices as well as a cultural shift within the business, embracing new ideas and technologies that can enhance their appeal and operational efficiency. They need to reimagine their strategies, form new partnerships, and find fresh revenue streams, ensuring they add value to their communities.

Classification Criteria for Visionary and Drifter Businesses

To independently assess businesses along the Value Proposition axis, focusing on profitability and growth while distinguishing between 'Visionary' and 'Drifter' entities, the following externally observable Key Performance Indicators (KPIs) can be employed:

- Market Expansion: Assessing the expansion into new markets or customer segments. Visionary businesses often explore and penetrate new markets, while Drifters usually maintain their existing market base.
- Product or Service Diversification: Monitoring the introduction of new products or services. Visionary businesses frequently innovate their offerings, unlike Drifter businesses, which tend to stick to their traditional range.
- Physical Expansion: Note any visible changes in the size or number of business locations. Visionary businesses often show physical growth through additional or expanded locations, while Drifters typically do not change in size.
- Customer Traffic Upward Trends: Observe the flow of customers over time. An increase in customer traffic can indicate a Visionary business experiencing growth, whereas a steady or declining flow might suggest a Drifter business.
- Visibility of Promotional Activities: Monitor the presence and frequency of marketing campaigns, special offers, or events. Visionary businesses often engage more in promotional activities to attract customers.

- Adoption of New Technologies: Noting the use of modern technologies, such as digital payment systems, online ordering, or advanced equipment. Visionary businesses are more likely to adopt new technologies compared to Drifters.

An example business in the Visionary-Drifter spectrum is Faubourg, a French restaurant located in Montclair, NJ. They recently had a huge capital investment to expand their seating area and created several different spaces, offering a terrace, cocktail bar, and formal dining room. They are consistently a hot ticket in town, with a significant percentage of its 209,300 visitors during 2023 coming from five to ten miles, with an upward trend of 6.8% year-over-year and 128% YO3Y. It qualifies as a Visionary.

Market Expansion	H
Product of Service Diversification	H
Physical Expansion	H
Foot Traffic Upward Trend	H
Visibility of Promotional Activities	H
Adoption of New Technology	L

Main Street Renaissance: Overcoming Drifter Challenges and Boosting Visionary Success

Understanding the dichotomy between Drifter and Visionary businesses will help in promoting sustainable economic growth and value creation in our main streets and downtowns. Drifter businesses, often established with conventional models and operating as they have since their inception, face the pressing challenge of adapting to today's evolving markets. Their primary struggle lies in overcoming inertia in business practices, which hinders their ability to respond to changing consumer preferences and emerging market trends.

To effectively position Main Street for its transition to the Experience Economy, transforming Drifter businesses into entities that are more adaptable and responsive to market dynamics is key. This task involves personalized consultations to modernize business models, training in digital tools and marketing strategies, and guidance on upgrading experiences. The goal is to shift these businesses from their stagnant state, characterized by conventional, less adaptable models, to more complex, enterprising operations that are open to partnerships and have the necessary capacity to see the win-win outcome of a deep commitment with improving the quality of the public realm and the experience of customers and visitors.

At the district level, creating an environment conducive to change and innovation is paramount. Initiatives like business incubators, shared marketing platforms, community events, and collaborative opportunities initiated by Place managers can inspire even the most static businesses to realign their strategies with the evolving market.

On the other end of the spectrum, Visionary businesses, with their complex, adaptable models and entrepreneurial spirit, are naturally positioned to lead the charge into the Experience Economy. Their active engagement in branding, marketing, and innovative design sets them apart as industry trendsetters. These businesses understand the importance of strong brand identity in today's competitive marketplace. They are at the forefront of exploring new market opportunities and setting trends.

The best help for Visionary businesses, known for their market adaptability and profitability, is a continued effort to make Main Street a more business-friendly environment. Visionary businesses can make a tremendous contribution by guiding and mentoring Drifters, creating a mutually beneficial situation that adds value to the entire Main Street ecosystem.

Focusing on creating massive value as a driver of a place's attractiveness will change the dynamics of Main Street revitalization and position Main Street to embrace the myriad opportunities that the Experience Economy and an ever-evolving marketplace bring.

Brand Cohesion Axis: Delivering the Magic

The Brand Cohesion axis offers a comprehensive view of how a business delivers its service to its customers. It emphasizes the need for creativity and exceptional hospitality, infused in major operational decisions as well as in evolving aspects such as store design, service delivery, and on-site, daily operational choices. This axis distinguishes itself from the Visionary-Drifter axis, which deals with how businesses design their strategic path toward efficiency, profitability, and growth. The distinction explains the difference between a business's overarching strategic plan and the tactical, daily actions that shape customer interaction, engagement, and experience.

The quality of the physical store design is instrumental in conveying the business's message and mission. The architectural layout, interior design, and overall aesthetic of a store align the brand's identity and magnify the experience. Effective store design attracts customers but also triggers a transformative experience that reinforces the brand's values, contributing significantly to the business's marketing and sales strategies. It needs to be flexible, adaptable, and conducive to hosting the daily magic show of service delivery and customer engagement.

Another critical element is the set of protocols and behaviors that employees are trained to follow. From customer service guidelines for brand representation to the embodiment of the brand's ethos in every interaction, well-defined employee protocols ensure consistent service quality, strengthen customer loyalty, and amplify the brand's image. Disney's guidance regarding hiring, training, and deploying their "cast," as well as the value that they add and the support that they give, ensure a fantastic employee experience.

Service design is the essential aspect of business operations on this axis insofar as it includes the setting, customer service practices, and store activation. Successful implementation of Service design strategically creates and organizes all service elements – from the texture of the floors to the music, to the quality of silverware to the way the customers are handed their bags after payment – to improve quality and interaction between the service provider and customers.

This encompasses the entire service delivery process, making it user-friendly, efficient, and effective, and includes all customer touchpoints from the initial engagement to the final service experience. The integration of store design and employee protocols with service design and operational decisions creates a cohesive brand narrative. Cohesion enhances the experience while amplifying marketing efforts, turning a well-designed store and exemplary employee conduct into powerful tools for attracting customers and driving sales. The goal is to provide a seamless, enjoyable, and valuable journey for the customer, thereby enhancing business performance and customer satisfaction.

The two types in this axis are Couplers and Dampers.

Couplers: Pioneering Adaptability and Growth

Coupler businesses stand out for their innovation, adaptability, and common practice of aligning every facet of their operation with their brand's mission and message. These enterprises are often in tune with market trends, adjusting their strategies, services, and even their physical space to meet evolving customer demands. Their agility stems from a forward-thinking mindset, the adaptability to market shifts, and a proactive, flexible approach to service design, ensuring they remain relevant in ever-changing markets.

In these businesses, every detail of the customer journey is meticulously crafted for maximum engagement and satisfaction. This includes the operational and service aspects and the physical design elements like layout, lighting, and ambiance, as well as the intentional protocols followed by employees during customer interactions. Their efforts extend to all channels, from physical storefronts to digital platforms, guaranteeing a consistent, cohesive, and enjoyable experience.

Hospitality businesses often exemplify this Coupler model. They leverage every customer interaction as an opportunity to impress and create memorable experiences. They meticulously refine all aspects of their service, from the inviting atmosphere of their space to the personal touches in customer interactions, to continuously set a high standard. A successful technique for local businesses in Main Street and downtown areas involves the cohesive management of branding, design, and service delivery, which will distinguish local shops from the insipid convenience and pricing of online and national chain retailers.

Insights garnered from successful hospitality ventures offer a blueprint for Main Street businesses, accentuating the significance of integrating hospitality into all customer service facets and transforming every interaction into an experience of warmth and welcome.

Dampers: Maintaining Consistency in a Changing World

Damper businesses represent the other end of the Brand Cohesion Axis, marked by their challenges in aligning the different aspects of their operation and service delivery with their brand's mission and message. These businesses often exhibit a firm adherence to established procedures despite a limited record of successful outcomes, which can be a recipe for stagnation and a disconnect with evolving market trends. Their approach to business often lacks the agility and forward-thinking mindset necessary to adapt to market shifts and best practices, resulting in operational and service designs that may not adequately reflect current customer expectations or needs.

Engaging, selling customer journeys require an environment that invites a transformative process. Businesses that excel at creating them are those that take full advantage of the time their customers spend in their stores. In Damper businesses, there is a disconnection that can be attributed to various aspects of their operation, including outdated or misaligned store layouts, lighting, and ambiance, as well as employee protocols that do not effectively represent the brand ethos or enhance customer interactions. Their efforts may need to be more consistent across different channels, leading to a customer experience that is less cohesive and enjoyable.

Typically, these businesses include long-standing family enterprises or local single-crew service businesses with set operational patterns and services that are hesitant to adopt new technologies or update their value propositions. Their focus on maintaining established ways of operating often overshadows the need to innovate and refresh their operation to meet current market demands. The result is an experience that needs to catch up to the dynamic and inviting nature offered by businesses that provide a consistent adherence to good design, branding, values, and mission.

Damper businesses face the challenge of modernizing and realigning their operations, physical space, and employee engagement strategies to create a more harmonized and appealing customer journey.

Classification Criteria for Couplers and Dampers

To assess businesses on the Brand Cohesion axis, focusing on how well they align their service delivery, operational decisions, and store layout with their brand, the following externally observable Key Performance Indicators (KPIs) can be utilized to distinguish between 'Coupler' and 'Damper' businesses:

- Brand Consistency Across Channels: Observe the uniformity of the brand's messaging and visual identity across various platforms, including physical storefronts, websites, and social media. Couplers maintain a consistent brand image across all channels.
- Brand and Setting Design Alignment: Assess how well the physical appearance of the business reflects the brand's ethos. Couplers often have a well-designed storefront and interior that resonates with their brand identity.
- Employee-Customer Interaction Quality: Note the nature of interactions between employees and customers. In Coupler businesses, staff interactions typically reflect the brand's values and mission.
- Customer Engagement and Response: Observe customer engagement within the store and response to the business's promotions or events. High engagement levels can indicate a Coupler business that successfully connects with its customers.
- Innovative Use of Space and Technology: Look for innovative adaptations in the use of space and technology that align with the brand. Coupler businesses often integrate technology and design elements that enhance the brand experience.
- Community Engagement and Partnerships: Observe the business's involvement in local events, collaborations with other businesses, or sponsorship activities. Visionary

businesses are usually more active in community engagement and partnerships.

- Storefront and Interior Updates: Pay attention to changes in the storefront, interior design, or overall presentation. Regular updates may indicate a Visionary business adapting to current trends and customer preferences.

An example business in the Coupler-Damper spectrum is DollyMoo, a hand-made soaps and cosmetics shop located in Montclair, NJ. They manage their social media with strict cohesion to their brand voice and values and keep that mood throughout the store. Every employee is engaged and supports the brand values. Reviews and integration with their customers are visible through social media posts and attendance at events and gatherings. DollyMoo's brand is consistent with a low-tech environment, so there is not much technology available in store, although they use digital apps extensively. They often interact with other stores in town and with the community and participate in events, do pop-ups, and entertain in their store. They have a tiny footprint, yet manage to keep it decorated for each season and important time of year. It qualifies as a Coupler.

Brand Consistency Across Channels and Store Design	H
Employee-Customer Interaction Quality	H
Customer Engagement and Response	H
Innovative Use of Space and Technology	L
Community Engagement and Partnerships	H
Storefront and Interior Updates	H

Brand Harmony: Navigating Cohesion and Fragmentation

The interaction between cohesion and fragmentation shapes the landscape of Main Street. Couplers drive innovation and growth, continually adapting to stay relevant and competitive. In contrast, Dampers offer familiarity but may need help to keep pace with market changes.

Their different contributions to the quality of the public realm manifest in the attractiveness of their block, district, and town.

To cultivate a thriving business ecosystem, a trend toward cohesiveness between brand, values, and message throughout the district will make a difference at both the individual business level and at the district. Encouraging collaborations or partnerships between the two types of businesses could yield innovative solutions that spread the need for cohesiveness.

The key to transforming Damper businesses lies in tailored interventions, which can include workshops on digital literacy, mentorship programs pairing them with more technologically savvy businesses, or community-led initiatives that celebrate traditional business models while gently nudging them toward modernization.

Supporting Coupler Growth

For Couplers on Main Street, the focus should be on maintaining a connection with the community while providing stellar service in beautifully designed stores and creating a service culture that defines and transcends the boundaries of their district. These principles must align with the needs and values of the local community if a business is to contribute to building up civic pride, a key component of vital, prosperous cities and towns.

To effectively enhance our downtown areas, it's important to strike a delicate balance between upgrading individual businesses' service and setting design while making sure the community's installed capacity supports the market and industry. Place management organizations are a defining actor in this context. They must bridge the gaps, ensuring the community can effortlessly host outstanding businesses, which in turn contribute significantly to the neighborhood's vitality and well-being.

Success on the Brand Cohesion Axis is measured in how its message is received by the community that patronizes the business. For Couplers, success might lie in their ability to innovate in design and service delivery on an ongoing basis. For Dampers, success could be found in a path to reconcile their essence and standing in the community with the public-facing components of design and service delivery.

Preparing Main Street For Tomorrow

The aspects covered by these three axes serve as a barometer for how well-prepared Main Street and downtown businesses are for the future. Main Street is in constant evolution. Understanding where businesses fall on this spectrum can help place managers identify areas for improvement and growth where long-term vision is complemented with immediate responsiveness.

Communities and business leaders can use this understanding to cultivate an environment where cohesion is valued at both the individual business and district level, leading to a unique Main Street with a strong identity and high civic pride, which is economically robust, culturally rich, and adaptable to the demands of the future.

Chapter 5. Decoding Main Street

The categorization of Main Street businesses, as outlined in the text, is divided into three axes: Creators-Seekers, Drifter-Visionary, and Coupler-Damper. This categorization is the foundational layer in our understanding of the diverse business landscape and the multifaceted nature of individual businesses on Main Street.

The next steps in the process are to identify distinct business types and develop strategies that enhance their potential, ensuring they contribute effectively to the district's vitality. Each axis represents specific characteristics and challenges of the businesses, by themselves incapable of codifying business types and enabling successful support.

In the following analysis, we explore the various business types that emerge from the possible combinations within our three-axis classification system to gain a better understanding of the complex nature of Main Street businesses. Each type has unique strengths and needs, which, properly addressed, can solve recurring issues of unpredictable returns on investments and inefficient resource allocation.

The primary objective of grouping businesses into types is to guarantee that each one, irrespective of its categorization, obtains the necessary guidance and support to create value and prosper.

A Catalog of Local Businesses

Each business type below represents a unique set of opportunities and challenges. The support strategies we propose in the following sections will focus on leveraging the strengths of each type while addressing any specific areas that require improvement or transformation. Here are the possible business type combinations and tailored strategies for each:

Creator-Visionary-Coupler: Creator businesses, highly adaptable leaders in their markets, are known for their innovative and unique offerings. They excel in aligning their products or services flawlessly with market demands, boasting a value proposition that is both profitable and appealing. These businesses are distinguished by their entrepreneurial spirit, allowing them to adapt to market shifts in a nimble, agile manner. Their dynamic approach to business operations and a keen eye for market trends ensure they stay ahead in a competitive landscape. **Strategy:** Encourage the adoption of an extraordinary customer service ethic to ensure their transformation into full-blown hospitality businesses.

Creator-Drifter-Coupler: These are typically cherished local staples, preferred for their enduring presence, familiar, beloved offer, and traditional appeal. Though they may need to update their value proposition, they still maintain a charming, solid service delivery that banks on the patina of time despite not implementing the latest trends and best practices. Their branding is their longevity. Their impact in crafting and maintaining the local identity and as living historical landmarks is outsized. These businesses exemplify stability and a consistent product-market fit. Their most significant challenge is to upgrade their value proposition to ensure their continuity. The fundamental **strategy** for these businesses involves leveraging the strength of their products and services to nurture a loyal following that transcends the local, allowing them to climb to the top of their market and ensuring financial sustainability.

Creator-Drifter-Damper: These businesses typically lack a value-generating profit mechanism and maintain operational practices in need of an upgrade. They often need more capacity for implementing outstanding service design and operational practices despite offering reasonably well-demanded products or services. They strike a balance between delivering reliable, though sometimes outdated, service, finding profitability, and innovating to stay attuned to market shifts and customer preferences. The **strategy** for these businesses begins with designing a viable organizational blueprint and then diving into the different aspects of service delivery and design.

The Creator-Drifter-Damper type includes a category that could be studied on its own: the Hobby businesses, which are often impaired by business models that are not conducive to growth or contribute to making Main Street great. Hobby businesses have outstanding, high-quality products, and are typically open for very few, odd hours, and despite hefty investments, appropriate branding, and setting design, their closed doors and dark shops detract from the overall vitality of the place. They maintained displays and clean facades despite a low business volume, which suggests that they do not rely on their on-site operations for funding the business. Good ideas and good design ought to be celebrated, yet a constant search for the best incentives to keep these businesses open for more regular, longer hours is probably the best way forward.

Creator-Visionary-Damper: Businesses distinctive for their trendsetting and appealing products or services, coupled with a strong market presence. They demonstrate optimal product-market fit and an innovative business model, which positions them as leaders in their industry. However, these businesses tend to adhere to conventional operational methods and refrain from significant investments in their store, branding, and marketing, showing a preference for product over delivery. The need for more organization and consistency in their operations can sometimes limit their ability to craft a more complex offer. **Strategy:** An overhaul of their operations, setting, and service design, which is a daunting task, however attainable on account of their vision and dynamism.

Seeker-Visionary-Coupler: these businesses are characterized by their innovative concepts and excellently designed service delivery models. They have yet to identify a unique idea or niche in the market but have developed a service model that is both efficient and customer-focused. However, despite their creative approach and operational agility, they need help in achieving a solid product-market fit. This discrepancy often results from a gap between their innovative offerings and the market's readiness or ability to embrace such changes. **Strategy:** these businesses need to realign their innovative concepts with market demand, continually adapt their strategy, and reevaluate their target audience to ensure a better alignment with consumer needs and preferences.

Seeker-Drifter-Coupler: Despite some innovative elements, especially in their service design and operations, these businesses face decline, overshadowed by static structures and an inability to find a good market fit. They face a complex scenario, requiring strategic rethinking to invigorate their revenue framework and market fit. **Strategy:** Translate the passion they put into the creation of their organizational and service models into finding a problem to solve with a new product and then create a sustainable business architecture to ensure profitability.

Seeker-Visionary-Damper: Businesses that have not found a good product-market fit and have a conventional, bland approach to service delivery. Even a slight decline in revenue could threaten the sustainability of the company. Its value proposition needs to be reinforced to sustain the other two pillars. **Strategy:** Leverage the creativity that they used to design the business model to find a better product-market fit and then revamp operations and delivery.

Seeker-Drifter-Damper: The most threatened category, these businesses are hindered by poor product-market fit and face declining revenue and dwindling customer interest. This challenging scenario often leads to low morale and little incentive for change, making it imperative to address their challenges and strategically rejuvenate the way they do business. Typical entities of this type are entry-level, subsistence businesses such as neighborhood hair or nail salons or small bodegas. **Strategy:** Revisit the early stages, starting with a value proposition that leads to the creation of a new viable prototype, redesigning the profit mechanism to fit, and focusing on the basic tenets of service to upgrade the experience.

Redefining Main Street's DNA

This comprehensive classification of business types guides us to understand specific issues affecting the diverse array of businesses in our downtowns and main streets. Designing and implementing strategies to tackle issues unique to each business type will maximize the value they can create and their contribution to the local economy.

We now shift our focus to the nature of each business type and the rationale behind concentrating revitalization efforts on the highest-rated ones. Such a path can enhance the overall context for mid-tier businesses to align their practices with proven avenues for profitability and value creation. It also establishes a solid foundation for providing much-needed assistance for those at the lower end of the spectrum.

As we explore deeper, we will uncover the interconnectedness within Main Street's diverse business ecosystem and examine the dynamics of collaborative ecosystem building, while focusing support in the areas with the most return potential. We will show how partnering with top-tier businesses to harness their contributions to the quality of the public realm can uplift the entire community, setting the stage for enduring success and vibrancy in the heart of our towns and cities.

The essence of this book's central thesis is profoundly rooted in the enormous potential that local organizations have to identify, curate, and attract top-tier independent local businesses and to undertake what is known as "Place Management" – the strategic and collaborative process aimed at creating and maintaining high-quality public spaces that are beautiful, functional, and inviting.

The strategic approach we propose relies on our ability to recognize the local actors that inherently resonate with their customers and add value to their entire industry, exemplifying a blend of market acumen and innovative prowess. The importance of the proposition in "Main Street Mavericks" lies in identifying potential mentors and mentees, and carefully cultivating relationships among all businesses in the Main Street ecosystem. In the end, we create a synergy that transcends individual success.

Identifying our benchmark businesses is akin to pinpointing the catalysts for communal and economic transformation. Curating their presence and attracting them to the forefront of Main Street initiatives means leveraging their potential to inspire and lead.

We have categorized local businesses into three distinct levels based on their product-market alignment, the flexibility and sophistication of their revenue frameworks, and their emphasis on operational efficiency and service excellence. These categories are known as the Attractors, the Stabilizers, and the Decliners.

Market Resonance, Business Evolution, and Excellence in Delivery

Businesses in the Attractor tier are distinguished by their exceptional mix of product-market fit, studied value proposition, vigorous and innovative business models, and excellent service delivery and design. Both types in this tier have a brand recognition that makes them preferred local as well as regional destinations. They attract the most foot traffic and drive most of the sales in a district because they offer transformative experiences with outstanding hospitality.

Attractors have successfully aligned their offerings with the needs and preferences of the market, enabling them to attract a substantial and loyal customer base. Featuring excellent design and outstanding service, they are highly vested in providing the best possible service delivery, which becomes a product itself, positioning these businesses as hospitality and experiential organizations.

The two types of businesses in the Attractor tier, the Creator-Visionary-Coupler and the Creator-Drifter-Coupler, have the highest visibility and highest potential for growth and adaptation. They are better positioned to lead the transition into the Experience Economy, further cementing their role as key drivers of economic vitality on Main Street.

Harnessing Hidden Strengths

The Stabilizer tier includes businesses that show promise and have moderate growth potential but require targeted support and development to realize their full capabilities. They may have elements of innovation or heritage value but need help building their operational dynamism and market positioning to match that of the Attractors. With the right strategies, such as market repositioning, operational improvements, or embracing new technologies, these businesses can ascend to the top tier.

In the realm of Stabilizers exhibiting moderate potential, we encounter a diverse set of types. The Creator-Visionary-Damper combination brings together forward-thinking, energetic, yet somewhat disjointed elements of design and service delivery. Similarly, the Creator-Drifter-Damper pairing combines progressive product development with a lagging business model and substandard delivery. On the other hand, the Seeker-Visionary-Coupler combination compensates for the exploratory phase of the Seeker with a dynamic and well-integrated framework. Finally, the Seeker-Drifter-Coupler type, which has employed the bulk of its resources in the delivery yet needs help with market fit and profitability.

Building On Modest Potential

Businesses in the Decliner tier are the most challenged, typically requiring special assistance to reverse a declining trajectory. While some targeted support might be beneficial to freshen up their image and service, the primary need for these businesses is an enhanced public realm and a more supportive economic environment so that those who demonstrate the skills and commitment can survive.

The focus for the Decliner tier is on elevating the community that supports them and finding the infrastructural improvements that can create a more conducive marketplace for all businesses. Developing a valuable public realm, improving local economic policies, and attracting a broader customer base are included in these strategies.

Businesses in this tier are often located in struggling neighborhoods that can benefit from these improvements and correspond to a particular category of subsistence businesses that eminently serve as alternative employment for vulnerable groups.

It is important to note that a large percentage of Decliners might be forced to close, despite the efforts in educational, economic, and contextual changes that their district managers, local governments, and other community members make to help them.

Decliners are identified as a specific segment of subsistence enterprises, offering alternative employment opportunities to marginalized demographics. Frequently situated in underprivileged areas, these businesses are positioned to gain significantly from enhancements to the physical infrastructure of their neighborhoods, as outlined in consultant analyses.

These changes can indirectly support these businesses, giving them a better chance to stabilize, rethink their value proposition, and potentially recover. However, it's essential to recognize that not all businesses in this tier will be able to adapt, and some may eventually close, despite the efforts in educational, economic, and contextual changes that their district managers, local governments, and other community members make to help them. The goal is to create a healthier overall economic environment that can sustain new and evolving businesses while offering the necessary support to those in the lower tier that have the potential to adapt and thrive.

Decliner businesses in need of significant support are the Seeker-Visionary-Damper and the Seeker-Drifter-Damper types. The latter type is typically made up of subsistence businesses sustained by a precarious symbiosis with its broader social and economic context.

What the Taxonomy Tells Us

Top-tier, Attractor businesses, thanks to their optimal positioning, create magnetic downtowns that draw more visitors and contribute to transforming their district into a destination. They are nestled in their districts, sharing geographical proximity with every other business in the vicinity. The foot traffic, attention, and purchasing power they bring are distributed across all business tiers.

While Attractors might only need a slight push to become experiential destinations, elevating every Main Street business is always the end goal. Recognizing the collective strength of the entire Main Street community is vital to achieve this. Every business, regardless of its type, can contribute to the district's vibrancy, diversity, and success. Hence, our strategy includes tailored support for businesses across all tiers, ensuring that assistance is customized to meet each entity's unique challenges and opportunities.

In the chapters that follow, we'll look deeper into the specifics of this strategy. We'll explore the collaborative creation of a local ecosystem where top-tier businesses share and nurture their counterparts and how to best structure the focus of local organizations in their role as catalysts for district-wide transformation. We will look into avenues for practical assistance for mid-tier and lower-tier businesses in overcoming their challenges and realizing their potential.

How To Analyze Your District

In the interest of working at different scales, which include the district, I'd like to expand the strategic framework to encompass district-wide development, categorizing areas into three distinct groupings, reflective of their economic vitality and growth potential: Experiential, Plateaued, and Struggling Districts. District managers dedicated to enhancing the quality of main streets or downtowns will benefit from a comprehensive analysis of the area's strengths, weaknesses, and opportunities. Such an analysis enables the development of informed strategies and targeted investments that optimize investment returns.

Experiential Districts, akin to the Attractor category, stand out for their dynamic business environments and high visitor engagement, driven by anchor businesses that excel in marrying product-market fit with innovative service delivery. These districts act as magnets, attracting top national and international brands, dedicated foot traffic seeking transformative experiences, and a stimulating atmosphere through unparalleled hospitality. They set a high bar for value creation, design, and community impact.

Plateaued Districts, where businesses in the Stabilizer tier are more prevalent, show growth potential and require strategic interventions to unlock their full capabilities. These areas benefit from initiatives aimed at strengthening business operations, market positioning, and embracing technological advancements to upgrade their status to Experiential Districts.

For local organizations, initiating basic Placemaking interventions serves as a catalyst for community collaboration and enhancing ownership of public spaces. Small steps contribute to increased civic pride and the development of a vibrant local ecosystem, where business and property owners unite with the shared objective of building up the local economy. Programs that rely on mentorship and collaborative initiatives facilitate the convergence of high-performing businesses with those still seeking to optimize their market impact.

Struggling Districts are often the host to the Decliner segment. They face significant challenges that necessitate concerted support from the public, private, and nonprofit sectors. Strategic enhancements to the built environment, streamlined permitting processes, and optimization of government touchpoints that impact the business climate can offer a lifeline to enterprises on the brink of closure.

The classification of districts into Experiential, Plateaued, and Struggling is not intended to stand alone. It is outlined in this short section to serve as a foundational reference for place managers. This framework can assist them in diagnosing the current state of their districts, guiding their strategic direction, and determining the optimal tactical interventions that will most effectively address the challenges and opportunities within their districts.

Chapter 6. Crafting The Collaborative Downtown

In tune with this age's interest in customization, this chapter will focus on the varied and nuanced ways in which partnerships and support structures for local businesses can be tailored, taking into account the unique combination of traits of each business type, as discussed before. I will share several stories directly from their protagonists to illustrate how local businesses, organizations, and communities can successfully work together to create a downtown that is both beloved and thriving. We will discuss how the different traits of each business type require distinct forms of support and partnership.

Having established the need for a tailored approach, and outlined the possible strategic directions stemming from the district classification, let's now look into the specific challenges and opportunities faced by different business tiers on Main Street.

Setting The Stage For Collaboration

As we review the Main Street economic landscape, we see that mid- and lower-tier businesses face distinct challenges. Stabilizers and Decliners often struggle with immediate issues like limited resources and low visibility. They also need help with more profound problems, such as difficulty adapting to market changes, creating demand for their product, and providing quality service. Understanding these specific hurdles is the first step in crafting effective support strategies.

We emphasize a nuanced, tiered approach to rejuvenating Main Street. We focus on the specific needs of each business type, creating avenues to maximize the impact of targeted investments made specifically where each tier needs them. The game-changing aspect of this strategy, however, is its focus on supporting the growth and increasing the visibility of Attractor businesses. These entities, with their significant sales and foot traffic, are instrumental in shaping the downtown experience. Their success and operational models provide valuable insights and benchmarks that other businesses can learn from.

While understanding and addressing the challenges of Stabilizers and Decliners includes them in writing the district's story, it's important to dissect the success stories of Attractor businesses, which have invaluable wisdom that businesses in other tiers can learn from.

Ask Not What Attractors Can Do For Others...

Attractor businesses, recognized for their success in drawing substantial sales and customer engagement, showcase a range of practices that can be invaluable for Stabilizers and Decliners. Central to their success is the delivery of an exceptional experience. Shifting focus beyond product or service quality to encompass the entire customer journey, thereby transforming the delivery into the product itself helps Attractors thrive and makes their wisdom part of a collaborative strategy involving mentoring and education.

A hallmark of Attractors is their effective branding and marketing strategies, characterized by a deep understanding of their target audience and the ability to craft an interesting brand story. To capitalize on this, Stabilizers and Decliners should refine their branding efforts, tailor their marketing strategies to unique niches, and engage customers through authentic storytelling.

Another significant aspect of Attractors' success is their adept use of technology. Establishing a robust online presence, leveraging social media for customer engagement, and utilizing data analytics for informed business decisions are among the strategies they employ.

Smaller businesses can adopt suitable technological tools to improve operational efficiency, expand their reach, and gather customer insights. Attractors often demonstrate a solid commitment to community engagement and local partnerships. They actively participate in events, collaborate with other businesses, and contribute to community causes. Other businesses in lower tiers can mirror this through active community participation, forming partnerships with neighboring businesses, and engaging in local initiatives, which can enhance their visibility and garner community support.

The final key area where Attractors excel is in their innovation, adaptability, and operational excellence. They are often at the forefront of industry innovation, responsive to market trends, and adaptable to changes in consumer preferences and technological advancements. Their innovative mindset and operational efficiency can be a model for Stabilizers and Decliners. By being open to new ideas, experimenting with new offerings, and optimizing their operations, these businesses can improve their cost-effectiveness and profitability. The goal for Stabilizers and Decliners is to avoid replicating Attractors exactly but to learn from their strategies and apply them in a way that aligns with their unique market environments and business contexts.

The diversity of businesses on Main Street means a single approach will only work for some. Instead, we propose tailored support structures. A very strong proposition with solid results is the establishment of mentorship programs that allow owners of successful businesses to share their expertise. Attractors have an immense wealth of knowledge and wisdom to share, which those in the lower tiers can identify and incorporate into their practices.

... But What Others Can Do For Main Street

Each business tier has inherent strengths and weaknesses. Recognizing and leveraging these is a decisive factor in a business' path to profitability. For example, a Stabilizer might have a strong local customer base but lack an online presence, an area where they can seek support or collaboration.

Stabilizer businesses, characterized by their moderate potential, often face a different array of challenges that limit their offer. Each business type in this tier might have strengths that are underleveraged due to their constraints. The main challenge for Stabilizers is to break out of their current state and embrace strategies that can hoist them up to the level of Attractors.

Collaborative strategies for Stabilizers should focus on market repositioning, operational enhancements, and the adoption of new technologies. A proven approach, often used in incubators abroad, involves pairing early-stage entrepreneurs with later-stage mentors to ensure that the messages are received on account of peer-to-peer communication. In tune with those experiences, pairing Stabilizers with Attractor businesses in mentorship programs, where they can learn about effective market strategies, operational efficiencies, and the integration of technology in business processes, is a promising strategy. Additionally, workshops and seminars led by successful Attractor business owners can provide Stabilizers with insights into innovative practices and new market trends, helping them to reposition their brand and optimize operations.

Decliners are in a precarious position due to insufficient product demand, an unprofitable organizational blueprint, and unimaginative delivery of services. One of the preeminent challenges for these businesses is to find ways to thrive in a struggling neighborhood or a challenging economic environment.

For Decliners, collaborative strategies are essential to improve the economic conditions where they operate. Engaging in community projects with local authorities and successful Attractors is one approach. Working together, they can slowly but steadily improve the neighborhood's appeal and attract a broader customer base through Placemaking, neighborhood watch programs, or public art initiatives.

Introducing Decliners to the successful business structures and practices of Attractors through community-led business incubation programs can provide vital learning opportunities. These programs can help Decliners reassess and adapt their value propositions, leveraging any inherent strengths, such as their duty as essential service providers for vulnerable groups in underinvested areas. The ultimate goal is to create a healthier economic environment that succeeds in sustaining existing businesses and attracting new and evolving enterprises, offering the necessary support for Decliners to stabilize and potentially recover.

Beyond the internal mechanics of individual business tiers, the support and involvement of local organizations builds up a business ecosystem where each business feels ownership and pride to contribute. In the following paragraphs, we explore how these entities can effectively boost business growth and collaboration.

The Nurturing Role of Local Organizations

While planning a new innovation district back in Quito, we hosted Professor Carlo Ratti of MIT and a few of his collaborators in the Senseable City Lab. Their focus was technology-led projects that could be tested and implemented in innovation districts all over the world. A bit advanced for the local ecosystem, yet intriguing enough to ruffle the feathers of local politicians and entrepreneurs.

Their presentation was as innovative and propositive as we had expected until one of them touched on the biggest setback he'd had while raising funds for a local district in his home country. Every round with major donors had several districts competing for funding. Their pitches were based on the strategic location of the district, the favorable weather, the kindness of their people, and their entrepreneurial spirit.

After the fifth similar pitch, he had to go back to his notes and change his before his turn, lest he be one of the dozens with nothing outstanding to offer. He had to pivot on the go and was generous enough to share the story so we'd have more time to focus on what made Quito stand out, that investors would find valuable, and make the decision to come.

Since that amusing morning almost a decade ago, my work has taken me to places with both wealthy and struggling downtowns, all over my base state of New Jersey and outside as well. Some struggle with safety and disinvestment, and others with property owners keeping prime real estate vacant, waiting for the national chain that will sign a long-term, triple net lease with increases tied to CPI or better. Their stories are varied, and the incentives that local businesses and property owners find valuable are unique, but the vast majority of local place managers have similar goals.

Place management organizations, such as Main Street managers, business improvement districts (BIDs), or private Economic Development organizations, strive to cultivate a supportive environment for businesses. Their work becomes particularly relevant in the collaborative revitalization of downtown areas, where their structure, scope, and reach positions them to bridge the gaps between businesses of different types and in different tiers.

The relevance of the tier system lies in its potential for investing resources in the most efficient possible way and reducing the number of opportunities that are left untapped. The classification of businesses into different types and along the different tiers is a tool that brings innovation into the Main Street industry. It has the potential of bringing innovative ways of looking at how different districts behave and tailoring the strategies to the specific needs of Experiential, Plateaued, and Struggling districts. This subject warrants a profound exploration in a separate book. Maybe I'll write it soon.

Regarding the current conversation, place managers optimally aligned with the hospitality and experiential strategies outlined in "Main Street Mavericks" are well aware of their standing along this spectrum. Their work is hard, and more often than not they need to educate business owners on issues that affect the shared spaces of the district, the way they are managed, and the rights of all businesses and members of the community. In the end, they all share a similar goal: to provide a great place that serves the shopping and socializing needs of their communities.

At a high level, the propositions of this book apply to every type of district. The collaborative nature of Main Street revitalization efforts remains unchanged regardless of the segment of the market where a given district and its businesses are located. The market trends towards seeking experiences and transformation will keep advancing and district managers must decide if working towards improving the quality of their public space, the hospitality of their businesses, and the experiences they offer would benefit their local economy, their district, and their businesses. Every downtown will have its Attractors, Stabilizers, and Decliners. The opportunities to collaborate and benefit from cross-pollination are there, despite the community's median income and the prevalence of businesses in either tier.

Through networking events, mentorship programs, masterclasses, and incubation programs that ensure lessons and wisdom are shared, local organizations can guide Stabilizers and Decliners to gain essential insights and knowledge about service, design, operations, or the actualization of both their value proposition and business model.

District management organizations are the driving force behind the advocacy for the health of the business ecosystem, a function that gains further importance in light of recent findings by the National Bureau of Economic Research. An NBER study from August 2022 reveals that regulatory constraints have induced a 5.8% decrease in innovation and growth. This insight highlights the urgency for local organizations to champion regulatory reform. Their involvement in streamlining processes, clarifying compliance requirements, and eliminating superfluous regulations can be game-changing for small businesses with single-digit profits within small operations. The advocacy of these organizations extends beyond just cost reduction; they are instrumental in cultivating an ecosystem that supports innovation and facilitates business growth.

This advocacy extends to infrastructure improvements and public realm enhancements, creating a more attractive and accessible district. Agencies such as District Marketing Organizations (DMOs) can lead robust marketing and promotional efforts to draw attention and traffic to the area, organizing events and digital campaigns that showcase the unique offerings of local businesses.

Organizing pooled resources, funding programs tailored to local business needs, and creating platforms and opportunities like mentoring programs and incubators can be particularly beneficial for businesses in lower tiers. A collaborative business environment is essential to the creation of shared value. Regular interactions and forums encourage the sharing of ideas and challenges. Networking support helps businesses implement recommendations from mentorship and incubation programs and unlocks additional opportunities for entrepreneurs to seize.

The principles of collaboration and mutual support among businesses lead us to the broader concept of Collaborative Main Street Revitalization. The concept encapsulates how multiplying these efforts can transform entire districts. The strategy that most effectively determines the roadmap is a clear, concise, measurable, and attainable plan to bring the business community together to talk about growth, entrepreneurship, and innovation.

Collaborative Revitalization

I went to college in a mid-sized, Liberal Arts school, where they offered a fabulous program in Hospitality. One of the most clever moves they made was making etiquette classes part of the core curriculum, ensuring that all alumni have a keen understanding of hospitality and service standards. The wisdom acquired from that program recently became useful at a Storefront Mastery consultation with a client. The issue we had set out to solve was the high rate of closure of Food and Beverage establishments within 2 years. We designed a cross-pollination program to pair them with top performers in the Hospitality industry in town, to allow them to experience what outstanding service is, and guide them in implementing similar standards in their operations.

An additional benefit from this innovative program is that mentor business owners realized they have teachable skills that can be shared either as a separate source of income or as a way to enhance their operations and employee experience.

Collaboration is the cornerstone of any revitalization effort that brings property owners, business owners, local government, nonprofits, and local place management organizations together, acting in the limited geographical area of a downtown or Main Street district. Any plans for collaborative Main Street revitalization should be designed to be a structured, step-by-step guide for rejuvenating urban centers that banks on the power of interaction and cross-pollination between Attractor, Stabilizer, and Decliner businesses.

Creating a collaborative culture among businesses within Main Street districts is fundamental for the advancement of shared growth and creating massive shared value. Just like our freshman businesses learning from the top restaurateurs and hoteliers in town, collaboration goes beyond mere coexistence; it's about championing a sense of place, community building, and mutual endorsement, where businesses and the organizations that support them actively work together to add value, create wealth and bring prosperity.

The collaborative spirit builds trust and understanding among business owners. Pooled resources can maximize the impact of marketing campaigns, collective events, and even shared services that can reduce costs and increase efficiency for all involved. Additionally, setting up a district-wide loyalty program or joint events can encourage cross-promotion and customer sharing, and creating a shared online platform or social media presence for the district can enhance its digital visibility and provide a collective voice. Leadership roles played by local organizations allow them to act as facilitators and catalysts for collaborative efforts, providing support and resources where needed.

This process goes beyond organizing community events and workshops and establishing collaborative projects, clinics, or incubators. It calls for the creation of a local platform, hinged by the work of place managers such as BIDs, chambers, DMOs, and other similar organizations, where Attractor businesses can share their expertise, lessons, and wisdom in building prototypes and iteration processes, perfecting business models, and designing exceptional stores and service delivery schemes. The goal is to create a sense of community and camaraderie between businesses and highlight the collective effort in the process of boosting civic pride, elevating the local business ecosystem, and transforming the district into a destination.

Destinations draw people in with the promise of unique experiences. While many successfully deliver on this promise, there's always room to polish these experiences further. At the heart of our proposal is the strategic harnessing of the influential power of Main Street Mavericks: those businesses designated as Attractors in our classification. These entities are the driving force behind the economic performance of a district. By tapping into the opportunities they create and sharing their valuable insights across the district, we can amplify our collective success. In the following chapter, we will examine a key support structure to ensure that the wisdom of these key players extends throughout the entire district.

Chapter 7. The Experiential Main Street

Back at Architecture School, I got a job designing an addition for a fascinating couple's home in downtown Savannah. William and Monique Armstrong were extraordinary people. She worked for the United Nations: worldly, sophisticated, well-versed in other cultures, and very elegant. William was a set designer for major movie productions. They had come to Savannah to work on a film that would be shot in the charming downtown streets.

It was my first brush with an outstanding "Employee Experience". I discovered new passions and interests, from wine and jazz to history and French cuisine. They trusted me with the keys to their stunning home on Chatham Square and, more importantly, their vast music collection. The most significant takeaway from that time, however, was the insight into William's work.

He was the artist in charge of transforming Barnard Street into a scene from the 1920s for a Robert Redford-directed movie. I observed as William and the crew created authentic storefronts, adapted streetlights, and staged modern roads to replicate the era. The scene came alive with actors, props, and lively street vendors, creating a purposeful "sidewalk ballet" that would have made Jane Jacobs proud.

This experience was transformative for me as a young designer, showing me the power of staging to create immersive experiences. I realized that design could shape human behavior. I got to witness first-hand how streets can metamorphose through simple gestures and become the stage for a play that has endless possibilities.

Until then, I had been unsure of the impact that design could have. It felt strange that we were required to design the path that the user would take and nudge their behavior in predetermined ways. Decades later, I can confidently say that though this may not be such a great trait for a home design, it has great potential to create unforgettable retail experiences.

Designing spaces for hospitality is akin to the executive production of a film. Each local business is a set where the stage is meticulously designed, with lighting, ambiance, and every minute detail working harmoniously to immerse customers in the story. Just as a film's production team collaborates to bring a script to life, business owners, designers, and staff members work together to create an authentic, engaging atmosphere that leaves a lasting impression. Every visit to a local business is transformed into a memorable, cinematic experience. Who doesn't love one of those?

This chapter marks a critical juncture in our discussion. It initiates an in-depth exploration of the experience economy, a key theme central to our book's objective. Our focus will be on transforming main street businesses and districts into exceptional hosts, capable of providing unrivaled experiences. We will revisit and build upon earlier mentions of the Experience Economy, expanding on principles and strategies specifically designed for Main Street enterprises. This comprehensive analysis aims to provide actionable insights for elevating the appeal and effectiveness of these businesses within the modern economic landscape.

The core of the section is a two-part game plan: first, to arm 'Attractor' businesses with the tools to excel in this challenging economy, and second, to reimagine the entire district as a lively, theater-like stage where every storefront has its moment in the spotlight.

Experience Economy Primer

To situate ourselves in the mindset of this chapter, it's important to first agree on a definition of the Main Street industry and identify the specific challenges that an upgrade to the Experience Economy might help solve. As understood here, Main Street is an economic sector focused on preservation-based revitalization and strengthening of traditional downtown and neighborhood commercial districts. It embodies a comprehensive approach to economic development and community revitalization, integrating aspects like economic development, local entrepreneurship, community engagement, and placemaking.

The Main Street movement, with a 40-plus-year history, started as a program of the National Trust for Historic Preservation and has evolved into the National Main Street Center, a subsidiary of the Trust, with over 1600 accredited districts across more than 40 states and an economic ecosystem that includes developers, consultants, service providers, academics, and hundreds of thousands of local businesses.[6]

---

[6] National Main Street Center website. mainstreet.org

There are tens of thousands of towns and cities with downtown districts that are not currently accredited Main Streets. These places face the same challenges and need to use the same toolkits to overcome them. They are seen, heard, included, and intended as part of the audience for whom this book is written. In many cases, unaccredited main streets are the core of very successful, beloved downtowns. Both showcase the power and resilience of a most American urban form, derived from the English High Streets.

Main Street businesses typically include a diverse mix of independent shops, services, and eateries, emphasizing local character, heritage, and a personalized experience. In recent years, a trend has emerged that props main street businesses, especially those with street-facing shopfronts, as stages where part of their work is to host and entertain.

Over the years, the Main Street industry has formed the backbone of dynamic, economically healthy communities by helping local businesses create value and preserve unique cultural and historic attributes. Nonetheless, Main Streets often face the challenge of economic competition, struggling to keep up with larger commercial entities like shopping malls and online retailers that offer a broader range of products, often at lower prices, and the added convenience of online shopping, which poses a significant challenge to traditional brick-and-mortar businesses.

These areas must balance the delicate task of preserving their rich historical and cultural heritage while keeping facilities, design, service delivery, and infrastructure updated to meet current market demands. However, constant upgrading of the store and service design can be both costly and complex. The success of Main Street relies heavily on consistent community engagement and support for attracting visitors, engaging residents, and encouraging both public and private sector investment. Maintaining this interest, involvement, and investment becomes increasingly challenging, particularly in the face of evolving demographics and economic conditions.

In the context of these evolving conditions, a shift beyond the traditional focus on goods and services has emerged. It emphasizes the importance of experiences as a distinct economic offering. In this "Experience Economy," value is perceived by customers as a function of the transformation they go through while in contact with the brand.

Joe Pine and James H. Gilmore developed their concept of the Experience Economy in their book of the same name, back in 1999. As discussed in Chapter 2, the concept revolves around the idea that in the current state of consumer behavior, businesses must create memorable events and deliver them spectacularly so that the delivery itself becomes the product.

Pine's and Gilmore's concept has increased in popularity, with almost 2 million results on Google. It has become essential for crafting business plans and designing service delivery in a context in which, according to PriceWaterhouseCoopers, 83% of customers are willing to pay a 16% premium for experience-based services, and companies that are leveraging the power of experiences earn 2.8 times the revenue of more conventional outfits[7].

---

7 PwC 2018 Experience is everything: Here's how to get it right.

A tremendous opportunity is emerging for Main Street businesses, which are uniquely positioned to offer exciting, unusual, and memorable experiences to their customers. Shifting their offerings to contemplate outstanding hospitality in the delivery of their products or services among a spectacular historical built environment offers a way to differentiate themselves in a competitive market marked by the constant and increasing onslaught from online and big box giants.

Experiences help local businesses encourage deeper connections with their community and clientele. Thus, a shift from traditional commerce to experiential offerings is decisive in the race to occupy a niche where local businesses in downtowns and main streets can easily beat the competition. It emphasizes that delivering unique, immersive, and memorable experiences can be more valuable than merely providing goods or services.

For these local establishments, embracing the Experience Economy represents a transformative approach to customer engagement. A shift in this direction can make a massive impact on businesses that thrive on unique, personal interactions, whether in the hospitality, service, or retail industries.

By creating personalized and memorable moments, they can significantly increase the quality of their offerings from simple transactions to memorable experiences. This outlook resonates deeply with Main Street businesses, where the emphasis is on community, individuality, and a unique personal touch. In such settings, experiences tailored to individual desires and interests can turn ordinary visits into memorable journeys, encouraging stronger customer allegiance and setting these businesses apart in a competitive market.

As we continue this exploration of the Experience Economy and the opportunities it offers for Main Street businesses, we turn our attention to a paragon of experiential design: Disney's Main Street USA.

I have my first recollection of visiting in the summer of 1980, and the magic was still very much alive last year as I took my six-year-old son, and we walked the same street as I had 40 years before. In the next section, we'll study the intricacies of Disney's Main Street USA, extracting valuable insights and strategies that can be adapted and applied to invigorate and enrich Main Street districts, magnifying their appeal and vibrancy.

This Is Your Brain on Disney

What if you could walk into a place that instantly made you feel happy, connected, and at ease? That is the magic that happens when we step into Disneyland's Main Street USA and feel an immediate sense of happiness, connection, and ease.

Disneyland isn't just any theme park attraction; it's a meticulously crafted environment that profoundly influences behavior and emotions. Charles Montgomery, in his book "The Happy City," along with our old acquaintance from earlier chapters, neuroscientist Paul Zak, experienced this wonder. They observed how the nostalgic and comforting design of Main Street, with its quaint architecture and engaging staff, contributes to a unique community spirit among visitors.

Disney's Main Street USA is very relevant to the design of real-world main streets all over the nation. Its importance emerges from its status as a prime example of immersive and customer-focused design. Main Streets are tourism drivers, and tourists seek experiences. They roam streets, enter shops, and dine in restaurants. Each one of those places contributes to the quality of the experience. A concerted effort where the community and the local organizations and businesses are aligned will make that experience unforgettable for both visitors and locals.

The sense of community that can be felt at Main Streets all over the country isn't merely an illusion in Disney's version. They understand the power of human connection and weave it into the very fabric of its space. Cast members, as they refer to their employees – note the theatrical reference – become friendly neighbors, engaging in warm conversation and dispensing genuine smiles. Even the music, a carefully chosen blend of nostalgic tunes and lively jingles, subtly encourages interaction, humming its infectious rhythm into the air.

To stage this emotional playground, Disney employs more than just charm. Montgomery highlights the strategic use of "micro-cues," subtle environmental stimuli that subconsciously nudge our behavior. The gentle curve of the street draws us toward welcoming storefronts, while strategically placed benches tempt us to linger and chat. Even the height of the buildings plays a role; those intentionally shortened upper stories create a sense of intimacy, making us feel closer to our fellow pedestrians.

The result is a potent cocktail of nostalgia, comfort, and connection. As Zak, a neuroscientist studying the biology of kindness, observed, Main Street triggers the release of oxytocin, the "love hormone" that enables empathy and trust. This potent mix encourages smiles, friendly greetings, and small acts of kindness – a far cry from the hurried anonymity of most city streets.

Utilizing substantial resources to research, implement, and refine advanced strategies, Disney can offer magical moments, forge emotional connections, and captivate guests. Displaying numerous staff, both in and out of costume, they meticulously cater to every aspect of the visitor experience, enhancing engagement at every stage. Main Streets are in a unique position to learn from and leverage these insights for their benefit.

The sheer quantity of resources, the access to the world's top scientific, design, and creative talent, and a century-old organizational commitment to never stop making improvements to their products are unattainable for local organizations, much less for individual local businesses. The lessons we can learn from Disney's experience are many, and several are available as publications from the Disney Institute. Implementing them in our downtowns and main streets is more a matter of will than budget.

Walt Disney called his creative team "Imagineers." They possess exceptional skills in design experimentation and in creating spaces that resonate deeply with visitors. Their work highlights the power of meticulous detail in crafting immersive environments. The Imagineers excel at transforming spaces into memorable experiences, where every element, from the layout to the tiniest decorative touch, contributes to a cohesive, enchanting story.

The term Imagineers is a portmanteau combining "imagination" and "engineering," reflecting the unique blend of creative artistry and technical know-how at the heart of Disney's design team. Imagineers are responsible for the creation and implementation of the innovative designs found in Disney theme parks, resorts, and attractions worldwide.

Disney Imagineers encompass a diverse range of disciplines, not limited to design alone. The team includes architects, engineers, lighting designers, graphic designers, audio technicians, special effects artists, and more. Each member contributes their specialized skills to the collective effort of creating immersive experiences. A multidisciplinary approach allows for the blending of creativity and technology, ensuring that every aspect of a Disney theme park, from the layout and attractions to the smallest details, contributes to a memorable and engaging visitor experience.

The Imagineers' mastery in crafting detailed, beloved spaces exemplifies the pinnacle of experiential design, setting standards in the industry for creating memorable and emotionally engaging environments.

Main Street USA has become a potent example for any business aiming to create a genuinely immersive, customer-centric experience. It reminds us that our environment isn't simply a backdrop; it's a silent conversation, constantly whispering to our emotions and influencing our actions.

Disney's experience of integrating storytelling seamlessly into the essence of public spaces and using design to nudge and encourage connection is relevant for Main Street businesses. It serves as a benchmark for how spaces where both community and individuality are celebrated can transform ordinary visits into memorable journeys and nurture customer loyalty in an increasingly competitive landscape.

The ingenuity and creativity of Disney's Imagineers provide a guiding beacon for Main Street place management entities. Just as the Imagineers expertly weave together various disciplines to create Disney's magical realms, local Main Street organizations can draw inspiration from their success story. By focusing on crafting every detail to enhance the overall experience, Main Street can be transformed into an immersive, emotionally engaging, attractive environment that offers opportunity to new and established, small and large businesses. Such an idea parallels the Imagineers' philosophy, where technical prowess meets imaginative design, setting the stage for memorable experiences that connect deeply with the community.

Strategies for Attractor Business Support

The Experience Economy represents a transformative shift in consumer behavior, where consumers place value beyond the products or services, into the transformational power of experiences. In this context, businesses thrive by creating memorable and Experiences that deeply connect and resonate with customers, transcending traditional transactional interactions.

The core idea of this section draws a parallel between individual self-improvement and the development of Main Street and downtown districts. Just as we, as individuals, focus on augmenting our strengths while addressing our weaknesses, this approach can be effectively scaled up to benefit business districts.

The strategy proposed here requires identifying and capitalizing on the strengths of the most successful businesses – those in the upper echelons in terms of product, profit, and operations, which attract significant foot traffic and drive sales. These businesses are the pillars upon which we can build the district's image and success. Concurrently, the broader strategy embraces a collaborative approach, aimed at elevating the performance of other businesses through cross-pollination of ideas and practices.

The structure of support for Attractors on Main Street – those ideally positioned to evolve into the Experience Economy – will spearhead a positive transformation of their entire districts. These well-rounded businesses naturally lean towards adopting new technologies and devising innovative processes that help them find an exceptional market fit and a critical mass of followers and advocates, setting the stage for a more experiential approach to business.

This strategy encompasses two complementary components: First, assisting businesses in envisioning and designing their setting and service delivery to create engaging experiences. Second, systematizing the roadmap to amplify the synergy between businesses and the public realm. The ensuing implementation includes nurturing a distinct local brand by capitalizing on the unique attributes and strengths of the businesses as branding assets and cultivating a growth-minded, value-creating environment that both complements and supports the local business community.

Part 1: Executive Production Of The In-Store Experience

Partnerships between Attractors and local Place Management teams can be the catalysts in the shift toward the Experience Economy within downtown areas. These collaborations are instrumental in introducing Attractors to innovative business models and cutting-edge technologies. Support offered can take various forms, including financial incentives for in-store and outdoor space activation or mentorship programs focused on exceptional hospitality practices.

In-store and outdoor space activation for businesses transitioning into the Experience Economy involves much production to transform physical spaces and stage them to host engaging, memorable experiences for customers. The phases in this process are Planning, Design, Technology, Bricks & Clicks, The Digital Storefront, HAL 9000 (aka Artificial Intelligence), Staff Training, Marketing, Activation, Collaboration, and Hospitality. Let's look at each in detail.

Planning

To transform a conventional store into a captivating retail experience, we can create a plan based on Margaret Kerrison's approach to immersive storytelling. Here's a quick introduction to the fundamental steps in this process:

- **Understand Your Audience:** Choose your audience wisely, know who they are and what they seek in an experience.

- **Target Emotions:** Define the emotions you want to evoke during the interaction and afterward.
- **Theme, Time, and Place:** Set a clear theme that dictates the ambiance and period.
- **Craft Your Story:** Develop a riveting narrative that resonates with your audience.
- **Engagement Rules:** Outline how customers will interact within the space, including assigning them parts to play in the story.
- **Mood, Tone, and Enclosure:** Establish the overall feel, language, and type of spatial design that supports the theme.
- **Design and Layout:** Choose colors, materials, and lighting that align with the desired mood and theme.
- **Design the Journey:** Plan the customer's path, including flow, pauses, and key interaction points.
- **Transformative Moments:** Create significant moments, either educational or life-altering, that leave a lasting impact.
- **Soundscapes:** Integrate sound effects to enhance the atmosphere.
- **Authenticity:** Introduce elements, ideas, and processes so the experience feels genuine to the theme.
- **Emotional Anchors:** Provide props and cues that deepen the emotional connection.
- **Memorable Takeaways:** Identify elements that customers will remember most vividly.

Design

Transforming a business into an experiential destination is a blend of creativity and precision. Here, we offer actionable insights for visionary businesses to tackle this process. It serves as a guide through critical phases and elements, highlighting the importance of 'setting' in service delivery. Designing places that inspire is vital, as the optimal setting helps to narrate a business's unique story and connects with customers, kindling transformative experiences and ensuing customer loyalty.

Creating an immersive environment in a store presupposes the strategic arrangement of interior and exterior spaces to evoke a specific theme. Actions large and small impact the experience, including rearranging furniture, setting up theatrical lighting, changing floor textures, and establishing a specific playlist and room temperature. The customer's journey through the store is thoughtfully designed with a prearranged path, incorporating seating areas, deliberate pauses, focal points, and dynamic lighting changes. These elements work together to ensure that the customer experiences emotionally impactful moments, leaving a lasting impression as they move through the store in a designed, predictable manner.

As far as the design project, some essential elements to include are:

- **Conceptualization:** Begin by understanding the business's unique story and vision. This phase starts by hosting brainstorming sessions, mapping customer journeys, and identifying key themes and narratives that resonate with the business's brand and audience. If the brand is not up to date, a similar exercise that helps owners craft it from their unique story and vision will align the brand with the experience delivery.

- **Customer Journey:** In this design phase, layout planning requires creativity to craft an intuitive yet strategically guided experience for the customer. While the navigation through the store might feel natural to the shopper, in reality, every aspect is carefully predetermined by the designer. Thorough planning is aimed at showcasing products effectively and drawing attention to special offers. The goal is to lead customers on a journey from attention-grabbing to exiting back to the sidewalk that feels organic. Still, every step is designed to highlight essential products and areas, ensuring that nothing of importance is overlooked.

  The selection of thematic decorations calls for aesthetic enhancements to contribute to highlighting new products or showing the value of existing ones. Each decorative piece is carefully chosen to reflect the store's theme or brand narrative, creating a unified and engaging environment. Rigorous attention to detail in this selection ensures that customers are fully immersed in the retail experience, their attention captivated by the store's ambiance. The goal, as Joe Pine, author of The Experience Economy constantly reminds us, is to make our store worthy of the customer's time and have them spend it well while in the presence of our brand.

  Integrating technology in retail design goes beyond digital elements like touchscreens and augmented reality. The first goal is to take advantage of the novelty of technology to entice potential customers. The design of experiential stores incorporates sensory stimulations such as sound effects, ambient scents, tactile objects, and varied textures and materials to stimulate all five senses and make the experience more immersive. Such enhancements bridge the physical and digital realms, providing a unique, multi-sensory shopping experience.

In creating an immersive environment, the focus is on engaging all five senses to grab the user's full attention. Such an approach envelops customers in the store's unique world, making every visit a multi-dimensional journey deeply connected to the brand's essence. The use of sensory elements like dedicated floor textures, interactive materials, and even varying degrees of hardness in surfaces all contribute to a memorable, holistic experience that resonates with customers on multiple levels and triggers a transformation, which is the ultimate product that customers demand.

The concept of the entrance funnel in retail design, as detailed in "The Ten No BS Rules For Successful Storefront Design," is a strategy that focuses on creating an inviting and engaging entrance to the store by maximizing the immersion at the interaction point between the sidewalk and the storefront's entrance where grabbing the attention of passers-by is likeliest.

The entrance funnel is an essential touchpoint in the customer's journey through the store, serving as the customer's initial impression and experience of the retail space. It is crafted as an outdoor room that sets the tone of the business and spills over the design principles and strategies from the interior to the sidewalk area, using props, furniture, lighting, and other elements to grab attention and engage with the store.

The "decompression zone," as described by retail expert Paco Underhill, is a transitional space at the entrance of a store where customers adjust from the external environment to the interior retail space. It's at the zone where we set the tone for the shopping experience, helping customers shift their mindset from the distractions of the outside world to focus on the retail environment. It's often designed to be welcoming and calming, allowing customers a moment to acclimate and prepare for their shopping journey.

After decompression, the guided path through the store is about designing a customer journey that on top of being easy to navigate, leads customers strategically past essential products and displays, ensuring optimal exposure to the store's offerings.

Intensifying The final in-store interaction, the Send-Off involves careful planning to ensure it's not merely a transactional moment but the realization of the transformative part of the experience. This decisive touchpoint should incorporate a seamless payment process designed to minimize discomfort and enhance customer satisfaction. Additionally, the Send-Off can include opportunities for last-minute purchases, but more importantly, it should offer a unique parting gift or experience. The nature of the parting gift could range from several alternatives: first, a physical keepsake that resonates with the brand's ethos, such as a beautifully crafted product sample, customized merchandise, or a creatively packaged memento. The key is to ensure it's something unique that customers can't get elsewhere, making it a special reminder of their visit.

A second alternative is a *digital memento,* fit for today's digital age. Offering a virtual takeaway can be highly effective. The digital memento could range from an exclusive digital content piece, such as a personalized thank-you video, a digital coupon for future purchases, or an interactive app experience that extends the brand interaction beyond the physical store.

Perhaps the most important of the three, an *emotional connection,* is a most abstract yet significant parting gift. The goal is to create a lasting emotional impression. It could be achieved through a personalized farewell message, an engaging story related to the brand, or a unique in-store experience that leaves the customer feeling valued and connected to the brand.

- **Special Effects:** A big box pharmacy and a romantic Italian restaurant have very different lighting schemes, fixtures, and light bulbs. A very visible issue is the incorrect choice of light "temperature". Bright white lights with a high Kelvin degree rating above 5000K are not quaint, familiar, or romantic. Those warm, orange lights of 2000K or lower that create mood in restaurants are not comfortable for reading and other tasks. Businesses often overlook seemingly small details like lighting temperature, as well as other special effects that complete the experience, thus missing the chance to align the atmosphere with their brand's message. Lights, music, smell, a smile from the shopkeeper, and other elements are critical for bringing the design to life within the store and delivering a positive, unforgettable experience. Such an upgrade often includes some level of construction to implement a physical upgrade of the space. The more significant challenge in this phase is the delivery using top-notch craftsmanship, excellent quality materials, and impeccable attention to detail. Every feature, from the layout to the light fixtures, needs to reflect the envisioned design and the brand values, narrative, and mission.

Transforming a traditional store into an immersive, imagined world comes with its unique challenges and successes. The goal is to create an experience where the customer's journey leads to a significant transformation. Going beyond just selling products or services is a big ask from a small business. The reward they get from inviting customers to spend valuable and enjoyable time engaging with the brand, creating memorable stories, and turning each visit into a distinct narrative is exponentially larger than the purely transactional one of exchanging goods for money. This course of action -focusing on creating engaging and transformational experiences- represents the essence of sales in the experience economy.

Before proceeding to the next section, every business owner with a street-facing store on a main street or downtown, as well as the district managers, need to recognize that while crafting the physical environment builds the foundational layer of experiences, design is only one of the needed ingredients. The success of such settings hinges on the operational excellence, the dedication and skill of the employees, and the overall design of the services offered.

Technology

Great experiences are measured in their immersive capacity, i.e., the emotional engagement they can generate. Incorporating technology such as augmented reality, interactive displays, or personalized service tech to enhance customer interaction is optional. It does help, but the core of great experiences lies elsewhere. Effectively designed rooms with a straightforward narrative, clever and creative ways of conveying a message, and an appeal to all five senses require minimal high tech to be spectacular. Over-reliance on technology may cause a range of pitfalls for Main Street businesses. Key among these is the erosion of the authentic human experience. Main Street's charm lies in its ability to offer personalized, intimate interactions – something that technology alone cannot replicate. It is part of what makes them very hard to compete with and an edge that online shopping or large chain stores can never provide.

Genuine, meaningful interactions and a sense of connection and belonging characterize the authentic human experience. Authenticity is the lifeblood of Main Street's charm. The connection that a warm welcome from a store owner, the tactile joy of handmade products, and the sense of community that pervades the street create are inescapable ingredients of a transformative experience. Authenticity grounds and justifies the stories that give life to each product, the customized delivery of services, and the feeling that each visitor is not just a customer but a valued part of the local fabric.

In this context, the human touch is a must-have element that keeps Main Street authentic. While technology can enhance operational efficiency and reach, it can never replace the human elements of empathy, storytelling, and personal connection. Technology should be used judiciously to complement and augment these human interactions, not overshadow them.

We advocate for a balanced approach where technology is leveraged to support and enhance the human experience rather than replace it, ensuring that Main Street retains its unique charm.

Bricks & Clicks

We live increasingly in a digital realm, and Main Street needs to acknowledge the transition. Continuity throughout the brick-and-mortar and digital storefront ensures that the essence of a Main Street business is uniformly experienced, whether a customer walks into the store or visits its online counterpart. When adequately designed and managed, the authenticity of the physical store is seamlessly translated into the virtual experience.

A company's values and mission manifest in its branding, and the way it delivers its service through all channels either lives up to it and delivers the message properly, or fragments the perception of the business. The same visual system, color schemes, logos, and overall aesthetic should be consistent and support the transition from the real-life shopping experience to the online counterpart. A well designed visual system and brand style guide help build recognition and nurture trust among customers.

Similarly, the values and mission of the business should be palpable in both realms. Suppose a store prides itself on sustainability or community engagement. In that case, these values should be evident in every touchpoint, in the physical layout and products as well as in its digital content, social media, and online marketing.

The story of the business, often a compelling aspect of Main Street shops, also needs to be told with consistency. Whether it's the history behind a family-owned store or the journey of a handmade product, this narrative should be woven into both the in-store experience and the digital interface. Storytelling can be adapted for the digital space through blogs, social media posts, and digital storytelling tools, but the core message should remain the same.

Finally, there should be an integration of experiences. For instance, in-store events can be broadcasted online, or online promotions can be redeemed in-store. This strategy provides a cohesive narrative and creates a unified experience, encouraging customers to engage with both the physical and digital aspects of the business.

The Digital Storefront

Creating a digital storefront that effectively mirrors its physical counterpart involves a thoughtful translation of the store's tactile, visual, and emotional essence into the digital realm. Visually replicating the store's aesthetic is vital, employing high-quality images and videos that showcase products and interior designs and a website or e-commerce platform design that reflects the physical store's color scheme and style. The emotional connection of the store is conveyed through storytelling, sharing the history, product journeys, and values behind the brand with engaging content such as videos, customer stories, and blog posts. The focus of the digital storefront is the same as that of the brick-and-mortar storefront: conveying the message, inspiring engagement, and inviting people to share a lifestyle.

Choosing an e-commerce platform that aligns with and supports the business's operations, mission, and values is instrumental in translating the business' priorities into practices that reflect its values. Integration with native or marketplace-based platforms can broaden reach while maintaining brand consistency.

Integrating a seamless Point of Sale (POS) system to synchronize the inventory and customer experience between the physical and digital stores ensures consistency across platforms. The digital platform's user experience (UX) should be intuitive and mirror the physical store's ease of navigation, possibly incorporating features like virtual try-ons. Additionally, online customer service must embody the same personalized and efficient service found in the physical store, with future sections discussing staff training and integration of business culture, brand ethics, and voice in customer interaction protocols.

Exploring strategies for seamless integration between digital and physical realms implies using technology to enhance, not replace, the in-store experience. A trend that is growing exponentially is leveraging augmented reality (AR) features to complement physical products or services. AR can bridge the gap between online browsing and in-store shopping by allowing customers to virtually try on clothes or visualize products in their homes before purchasing.

Another strategy is implementing omnichannel retailing, where customers can seamlessly switch between online and offline channels. My local supermarket is a great example of this integration. To entice adoption of their shopping app, they place products in a prominent way, next to signs advertising "digital only" coupons. Customers activate the savings online and see them at the register.

Personalization goes a long way in integrating these realms. Utilizing customer data gathered both online and in-store can help tailor the shopping experience to individual preferences, whether it's through personalized product recommendations online or targeted promotions in the physical store.

Additionally, social media can be a bridge between the digital and physical worlds. Using platforms to showcase in-store events or special promotions can drive online audiences to visit physical locations and vice versa.

Consistent branding and storytelling across all platforms will ensure a unified customer journey, build trust, and contribute to the construction of a community of friends and advocates. Whether a customer interacts with the brand online or offline, they should feel a consistent brand presence and message, reinforcing the integrated experience.

HAL 9000

The portrayal of Artificial Intelligence (AI) in Hollywood often gravitates toward dramatic narratives, featuring scenarios such as futuristic automatons with destructive agendas, AI systems commandeering space expeditions, and individuals developing emotional connections with their digital operating systems. The depiction in broader media channels adopts an even more somber tone, highlighting concerns around the proliferation of deepfakes and the potential for identity theft, suggesting a reality where factual integrity is compromised, necessitating significant corrective measures.

The actual landscape of AI technology, despite its rapid advancement in recent months, remains far from achieving sentience. Currently, the predominant applications of AI are relatively mundane yet impactful, encompassing tasks such as composing social media content, assisting with academic writing, and producing creative works.

Innovative ideas often emerge from the most unexpected circumstances. While utilizing a music streaming application during a pause in my writing, I encountered a novel feature titled "DJ." This feature, powered by artificial intelligence (AI), functions as a personalized radio host, curating music selections based on individual tastes, historical preferences, and listening habits. As my personal DJ played a standard by Nina Simone, I started to think about how similar technological advancements could benefit local enterprises. Large Language Models, the technical classification for AI-driven text applications, when combined with voice synthesis, can create customized assistants capable of engaging with consumers through digital platforms, email communications, or directly on mobile devices. Artificial Intelligence models offer astounding potential for district managers, small businesses, and the entire Main Street industry to be more creative and productive.

We live in exciting times. The technological tools at our disposal have never been more accessible and the impact of a marketing or sales campaign managed by a small business owner equipped with a few free online apps can equal that of award-winning large agencies with dedicated staff and substantial resources.

Staff Training

Every part of customer interaction is an opportunity for a Main Street business to succeed. A play is only as captivating as its cast. In the same manner, Main Street businesses thrive on the kindness and skill of the shopkeepers. Staff turnover is often high, especially in Small Businesses. Hiring practices help to choose the optimal candidates to represent the business. Providing an exciting experience for employees, however, can go a long way in embedding the team within the business structure and counting on them to offer an immersive experience.

Businesses with strong value propositions, with clear messaging of their values and brand character, attract like-minded workers who more easily align with the overarching purpose. Using an indicator of service and workplace satisfaction that global consultants PriceWaterhouseCoopers call the "Return on Experience", adapted to the specific conditions of small, downtown businesses, ensures that each team member that has a fabulous employee experience performs their job efficiently and has an increased commitment with the creation of value.

Smaller, main street businesses range from single-crew to very small teams, where every member wears many hats. The best employee training strategy for such small units is to keep it loose. Choose great people based on attitude and personality, work on aligning the employee's goals with the business, inspire them to be the most loyal fans and vocal advocates, and give them room to grow and represent the business to the best of their capacity.

In this section, we explore some strategies and methods that have transformed ordinary staff training in larger businesses into an extraordinary experience that equips employees of innovative companies to dazzle and enchant. May these serve as a suggestion for smaller, local businesses that are intent on applying some best practices from larger entities. These are:

- **Comprehensive Orientation and Training:** Similar to Disney's approach, hotels such as Hilton and CitizenM provide extensive training covering job-specific skills as well as an in-depth understanding of the company's culture and values. Aligning staff organically with the organizational culture and the company's ethos ensures they are well-prepared for their tasks.
- **Role-Specific Training:** Disney staff, known as Cast Members, in reference to the hospitality nature of the parks, receive additional training tailored to their specific roles and locations. This specialized training ensures that each staff member is adept at their specific responsibilities and understands how they contribute to the larger narrative of the park.
- **Focus on Employee Experience:** Boosting the experience for workers builds up commitment leadership, promotes the adoption of systems and protocols, and ensures the delivery

of spectacular guest or customer experiences. According to PriceWaterhouseCoopers, companies that have a distinct experiential culture for employees, with leadership committed, have 1.9 times more revenue than comparable ones.

- **Skill Sharing:** Universal Orlando encourages cross-training among its team members, allowing employees to develop diverse skills and advance within the company. This method promotes employee growth and a deeper understanding of the company's operations, building a dynamic and guest-focused workforce. Adapting a similar cross-training approach could help Main Street businesses create versatile, skilled teams capable of delivering exceptional experiences to customers.
- **Additional Engaging Training:** Other quirky ways to align employees with the company's values might include interactive elements like walking tours, trivia games, or scavenger hunts. Gamifying the employee experience makes the learning process engaging and helps staff better understand and navigate their work environment.

Marketing

To explain what Marketing is and the extent to which local businesses need to understand and master all aspects, let's turn to entrepreneur and author Allan Dib's witty storytelling:

> *"Here's the simplest, most jargon-free, definition of marketing you're ever likely to come across: If the circus is coming to town and you paint a sign saying "Circus Coming to the showground Saturday," that's advertising. If you put the sign on the back*

> *of an elephant and walk it into town, that's promotion. If the elephant walks through the mayor's flower bed and the local newspaper writes a story about it, that's publicity. And if you get the mayor to laugh about it, that's public relations. If the town's citizens go to the circus, you show them the many entertainment booths, explain how much fun they'll have spending money at the booths, answer their questions and ultimately, they spend a lot at the circus, that's sales. And if you planned the whole thing, that's marketing."*

Allan Dib's quote from "The 1-page Marketing Plan" offers a simple yet effective analogy for understanding different marketing facets. This analogy can be contextualized in a Main Street revitalization scenario. Imagine Main Street as the venue for a unique local event. The quote's elements – advertising, promotion, publicity, public relations, sales, and marketing – can be applied to various strategies Main Street organizations might use to promote this event, each serving a distinct purpose in attracting visitors and creating value for the local economy.

Activation

Maximizing the use of commercial spaces is essential in today's retail environment, where Main Street America reports a downward trend on the footprint of local businesses which translates into opportunities for introducing collaborations, pop-ups, and complementary businesses that make better use of the space. Activating spaces transforms them into hubs of varied activities that extend beyond the usual offerings and times. This tactic ensures that at different hours of the day and on different days of the week, customers will encounter something new and surprising, adding an element of discovery to each visit.

There is something about active displays that gets people's attention and converts sidewalk foot traffic into footfall into the store. Creating a dynamic space that engages the public in diverse ways, from pop-up events to outdoor interactive experiences requires creativity above any other component. Here are some ideas for activating the front of commercial spaces:

- **Themed Events:** Organize events that resonate with the store's theme, such as product launches, cultural celebrations, or seasonal activities, to create an attractive, engaging atmosphere.
- **Interactive Workshops:** Conduct workshops that allow customers to interact with their own or their partners' products and learn new skills, strengthening their connection with the brand.
- **Live Performances:** Introduce live music, theater, or dance performances that complement the store's ambiance and entertain customers. A variation of this is immersive performances, which are not programmed, take the store in a seemingly impromptu manner, and generate direct interaction with customers.
- **Immersive Installations:** Create visually captivating installations or pop-up experiences that encourage customers to explore and engage with the space in new ways.

- **Storytelling Sessions:** Use storytelling to convey the brand's values and history, creating a deeper emotional connection with the audience.
- **Interactive Technology:** Incorporate augmented reality, virtual reality, or other interactive technologies to offer a unique and memorable shopping experience.

Collaboration

The spirit of innovation can enhance the presence of local businesses. Exploring the forward-thinking and groundbreaking strategies that can emerge from partnerships with local artists, crafters, local startups, or other businesses can bring a fresh, entrepreneurial perspective to traditional operational structures.

Adopting these modern, innovative tactics can redefine and energize the everyday business landscape of Main Street, creating unique, customer-focused experiences.

Below, we look at some practical ways to incorporate cutting-edge ideas and collaborative methods to revitalize local enterprises, transforming them into attractive, engaging community hubs:

- **Tech-Enabled Pop-Ups:** Partner with tech startups to create pop-up experiences showcasing cutting-edge technologies, like virtual reality demos or interactive digital art installations, offering a futuristic shopping experience.
- **Local Maker or Crafter Collaborations:** Collaborate with local makers or crafters for limited edition products,

blending traditional crafts with modern design, attracting niche markets.

- **Joint Venture Events:** Host joint events with nearby businesses, like a tech-themed street fair, combining technology demonstrations with local retail offerings.
- **Artist-in-Residence Programs:** Invite local artists for temporary residencies, where they create in-store, giving customers a behind-the-scenes look at the creative process and generating unique, purchasable art.
- **Startup Showcases:** Collaborate with local entrepreneurs to showcase their products or services within your space, providing a platform for emerging businesses and a fresh experience for customers.
- **Interactive Storefronts:** Work with local tech firms to develop interactive storefronts, turning window shopping into an engaging, gamified experience.
- **Community Incubator Spaces:** Create incubation spaces within the store where industry leaders and emerging entrepreneurs can collide, forging a dynamic, innovative, and collaborative ecosystem.

Hospitality

I have a mantra that I keep repeating to my clients: *Every Main Street business is a Hospitality business.* The phrase doesn't mean, of course, that Main Street is full of hotels. What it means is that in a uniquely complex economic climate where the opportunities for location-based innovation and growth are great but also are the challenges and threats they face, the way for local businesses to win is to carve a particular niche where the impeccable delivery of their products and services becomes the product, and customers prefer to buy experiences from downtown and Main Street businesses than to buy commodities from online retailers.

The toolkit for local businesses to become experiential is a hospitality playbook. Will Guidara's "Unreasonable Hospitality" concept offers a valuable framework for Attractor businesses on Main Street aiming to evolve into experiential destinations. This approach is centered on delivering customer service that goes far beyond the conventional, aiming to create standout, memorable experiences. For Main Street businesses, this translates into a deep focus on personalization and attention to detail. Personal touches like knowing customers by name, remembering their preferences, offering unexpected gestures or unique events that captivate customers, and customizing experiences can leave a lasting impression.

Whether they realize it or not, the niche where Main Street businesses can shine requires them to become experiential and excel in playing their part as the district's hosts. Suppose they concentrate on exceeding expectations, surprising and delighting their customers by offering outstanding hospitality within the appealing context of a diverse, walkable area. The unique combination of assets that Attractor businesses have makes it possible for them to carve a niche where they can have an unmatched advantage.

In a time when the convenience and price of corporate businesses wipe out those trying to compete in the same terms but without access to economies of scale, bottomless access to credit, and a pipeline for subsidies, tax credits, and other gifts, embracing Main Street's natural niche can be lifesaving.

The transition of Attractors into the Experience Economy, and the ensuing actions of their local place management organizations will significantly boost their communities' appeal, drawing substantial external attention. Increased visibility is instrumental in enriching top-tier businesses and also in inspiring many others to embrace a more experience-oriented model.

The newfound role of Attractor businesses as hospitality destinations -the "Attractor" designation is not casual- gives them the tools to craft immersive experiences, pursuing a culture of innovation throughout the entire district. Through these concerted efforts, Attractors become beacons of experiential commerce, inspiring and guiding other businesses in their transition towards more experience-centric models.

The embrace of Attractor businesses' platform as hosts for the entire district heralds a wave of economic prosperity marked by higher customer engagement, increased spending, and greater visibility for Main Street communities. It opens a window for place management entities like economic development agencies, BIDs, DMOs, and Chambers of Commerce to capitalize on this revitalized downtown ambiance. They can harness these improvements in creative marketing strategies, propelling local economies forward by investing in and activating the public realm. Part 2 of the strategy dives into how.

Part 2: Revitalizing the District as a 'Theater'

The revitalization of downtown districts into hubs of commerce and culture is a complex task with a long history of success and learning. The work of place management organizations, which include business improvement districts, main streets, downtown and redevelopment corporations, and other local agencies and nonprofits, has been invaluable in injecting vibrancy into streets.

This section looks into how strategic placemaking, effective branding, and active wayfinding promoted and sometimes implemented by these organizations can create cohesive, welcoming environments that support Creator businesses in upgrading to experiential offerings while elevating the context for Stabilizers and Decliners to take advantage of increased foot traffic and the target audience's purchasing power.

The performative approach to revitalizing public spaces highlights the contribution of these organizations in orchestrating the business community's response to large-scale events, thereby ensuring a transformative and lasting impact on the entire district, with a particular focus on aiding businesses in need of revitalization.

There are three main areas of focus for local organizations where they can contribute within their scope to a successful re-energizing of downtown streets:

Branding, Placemaking, and Active Wayfinding

Branding, in the context of a downtown or Main Street district, transcends traditional notions of logos and slogans. It's a vehicle for delivering the message of a unique identity that captures the essence of the area, resonating with both locals and visitors because locals ultimately create it. A district's identity should be a reflection of its history, culture, and aspirations, and it should celebrate the contributions of people and businesses, especially those Attractors that have risen to the status of local legends. Effective place branding creates a memorable image of the area, which attracts people by building up on an idea, setting it apart from other destinations. The story encapsulates the spirit of the district, consistent with its message and brand, signaling that they will find an unforgettable destination to experience and enjoy.

Placemaking is paramount in shaping the identity of a place. It goes beyond mere physical changes to the environment. Placemaking is about the collaborative creation of spaces that stimulate engagement, interaction, and a sense of community. Integrating aspects like public art, green spaces, and communal areas can beautify spaces and bring communities together. Placemaking connects the creative expressions of the community with the broader goals of the business district, adding a cultural and social dimension to the commercial hub.

Active wayfinding is an innovative blend of branding, signage, and Placemaking that implements physical interventions to serve as intuitive guidance systems within the public realm. Elements can include both physical signage and digital aids that help visitors navigate through the district. Active wayfinding enhances the overall experience of the area, encouraging exploration and discovery. It does the core job of directing foot traffic while inviting visitors into a discovery journey through the district, helping them uncover its stories, attractions, and hidden gems.

Together, these concepts – branding, placemaking, and active wayfinding – form a comprehensive strategy for transforming main streets and downtowns. They are tools that improve the aesthetic and functional aspects of a place and also deepen its character and connection with those who visit and inhabit it. A conscientious implementation of these strategies can elevate any district from a mere location to a spectacular destination.

Cluster building

Michael Porter is an economist, best known for his theories on economics, business strategy, and social causes. He's particularly famous for his work on the concept of industry clusters and the competitive advantage of nations. Porter's ideas have had a significant impact on modern business strategy and economic policy.

Porter's cluster concept delineates the geographical aggregation of interconnected firms, specialized suppliers, service providers, and related institutions within a specific sector. These clusters promote increased efficiency and productivity through proximity and interconnections. They encourage competition and cooperation, driving innovation and business growth.

Clusters also benefit from shared resources, such as a skilled, specialized labor pool and technological advancements. Promoting these clusters involves creating a supportive environment for businesses to collaborate, innovate, and access shared resources, emphasizing the overall competitiveness and appeal of the region.

In the context of Main Street, clusters manifest in the organic grouping of similar or complementary businesses. This condition emerges when businesses take advantage of proximity, naturally creating 'villages' that emerge without formal planning. Such clusters are hotbeds for synergies and attract more foot traffic, enriching the area's appeal.

Crafting a successful Main Street cluster strategy demands an approach that marries local charm with savvy business collaboration. Here's how to bring this vision to life:

- **Highlight Local Character and Specialty:** Emphasize the unique character and specialties of Main Street businesses, celebrating local culture and products.
- **Encourage Business Collaboration:** Facilitate partnerships and networks among Main Street businesses for joint promotions and events, enhancing collective attractiveness. Networking events and joint projects deliberately crafted to bring collaboration forth can be beneficial.

- **Tailored Marketing Strategies:** Develop marketing campaigns that reflect the unique vibe of Main Street, using social media, local events, and community outreach.
- **Engage Community and Local Government:** Collaborate with local stakeholders and authorities for support in initiatives that benefit the entire street.
- **Upgrade Infrastructure:** Invest in pedestrian-friendly features and communal spaces to make Main Street more accessible and welcoming.
- **Responsive Adaptation:** Continuously assess the performance of the cluster and adapt to changing market trends and community needs.

Marketing

Crafting a marketing plan for Main Street clusters transcends the realm of aiding individual businesses with their promotional efforts. Planning is approached from a higher level perspective that harnesses the collective power and unique characteristics of these clusters. This strategy is centered on highlighting the synergy and shared identity of the cluster's area, showcasing how each business, while distinct, contributes to the character and fabric of the district.

By leveraging the combined allure of the cluster's urban core, this approach aims to craft a gripping narrative that brands the area and also enhances its visibility. The goal is to strategically position the district as an attractive and diverse destination, drawing visitors and customers through a well-orchestrated promotional campaign. The process could entail organizing district-wide events, creating joint advertising initiatives, or employing social media strategies that celebrate the unique experiences each business offers, all while tying them back to the district's overarching identity and branding.

The place narrative-led marketing strategy ensures that the efforts resonate on a broader scale. The successful marketing plan relies on showcasing the district as an attractive, multifaceted destination, as opposed to a collection of fragmented promotions of individual businesses. The resulting increase in foot traffic and customer interest induces collaboration among the business community so that individual businesses benefit as well. The collective reward encourages business owners to view their neighbors not as competitors but as partners in creating a thriving, dynamic district.

Expanding on ideas for a marketing plan, we can integrate a powerful element inspired by storytelling expert Phil Eich's teachings: the best place marketing plan is showing human faces and telling human stories. Phil's company, Storyville, hinges its success on featuring legendary members of the community, allowing them to narrate their own stories in their authentic voices. Relying on human stories as the way of telling the place's story means actively seeking out individuals whose lives and work have shaped the character of the town. Typical local legends are long-standing business owners, local artists, historical figures, or even everyday residents who have a special connection to the area. Their stories, experiences, and personal journeys can be showcased through various mediums, such as video interviews, written profiles, podcasts, or live storytelling events.

The essence of this approach is to identify and showcase narratives that resonate with the authenticity and personal connection of the area. Locals, deeply embedded in the district's fabric, are the best scouts for these stories. They have an inherent ability to uncover compelling tales and experiences that define the spirit of the place. Harkening back to the Alan Dib quote about what Marketing is, part of the strategy is training local storytellers and elevating the training into an event that makes waves through the town.

Local marketing agencies are amplifiers of these voices, curating and promoting the stories to a broader audience. Through various mediums like video interviews, written profiles, and live events, these agencies broadcast the narratives, creating a synergy that increases the district's visibility and attractiveness. This strategic amplification is essential in drawing visitors and customers who are eager to experience the community's vibrancy and connect with the familiar faces and stories they have come to know.

The overarching aim of this strategy is to showcase the district as an attractive, multifaceted destination. The goal extends from promoting individual stores or services to celebrating the entire district as a foundry of stories. Each corner has a tale to tell, and every face has a story to share, creating a dynamic and engaging atmosphere.

By elevating the marketing plan beyond conventional methods, we can transform it into a powerful instrument for community building and engagement. Centered on the human spirit and the shared stories that unite the community, it boosts the district's visibility and deepens its unique identity. The district becomes a vibrant destination enriched by its human connections and diverse experiences, and not merely a collection of shops and services.

As we transition to the concluding chapter, "A Parting Gift," let us carry forward the essence of the Main Street Mavericks proposition: the belief that for the market to see the tremendous value that a place can offer, we need to tell the stories of people creating and building within that place. This belief informs our strategy and is a gift we give to every visitor and customer, a memorable experience that, like a cherished souvenir, stays with them long after they've left.

A Parting Gift

I first met Nicci Silva in an unexpected place – while playing with my three-year-old son at his daycare playground. Right next to it was a basement kitchen, part of what I still consider the most fragrant block in town, where DollyMoo was born. We started chatting through her kitchen window and became friends. This unique shop, nestled in the heart of Montclair, New Jersey, was created by Nicci and her sister in 2010. Their journey from experimenting with homemade products to opening a narrow yet enchanting DollyMoo storefront mirrors the transformative principles we've explored in this book.

The sisters' venture, supported by family and friends, evolved from selling at farmers' markets and festivals to establishing a physical presence in Montclair. Every aspect of their store, from its name – a term of endearment from their Greek grandmother – to the themed decorations and events they put up for each season and each holiday by masterfully arranging the storefront and staging their tiny store, exudes the love and spirituality that guide their journey. And let's not forget the killer playlist that constantly plays in the background, an eclectic mix that I find myself unable to stop listening to.

Today, Main Streets and downtowns face a seismic shift. The dominance of online shopping and large national chains, coupled with economic challenges like inflation, higher rents, and looming recessions, puts local businesses in a tough spot. Yet, fantastic local enterprises like DollyMoo stand as beacons of success, embracing the hospitality ethos and the experience economy with open arms. Their thrifty nature -they create their storefront displays themselves by hand and change them often; inherent authenticity and flair for implementing outstanding service and design resonate deeply with customers.

Small, local, bootstrapped shops have an edge in creating experiences that captivate their audience, often achieving this on a modest budget. They are the ones who will triumph.

I believe the story of DollyMoo, my favorite Attractor in town, illustrates the principles discussed throughout this book. Theirs is a tale of growth, experience, and community, showcasing the immense value local businesses add to the fabric of Main Street and the identity of their towns. They inspire their peers to strive for excellence, to aim higher, and to create 'magick,' as Nicci often spells it.

Welcome to the Experience Economy, where the charm and stories of local businesses with fabulous offerings, outstanding design, and excellent service delivery like DollyMoo make places unforgettable. Through the challenges and changes, your business will become an outstanding host, and your district will become an exceptional destination.

Welcome. I know you'll shine.